This book belongs to

_____

*a woman beautiful
in God's eyes.*

Beautiful in God's Eyes

Elizabeth George

HARVEST HOUSE PUBLISHERS
EUGENE, OREGON

Cover by *Terry Dugan Design, Minneapolis, Minnesota*

Acknowledgment

As always, thank you to my dear husband, Jim George, M.Div.,Th.M., for your able assistance, guidance, suggestions, and loving encouragement on this project.

BEAUTIFUL IN GOD'S EYES

In loving memory of
Lois George Onesti

Godly mother to my husband, Jim,
gracious mother-in-law to me,
loving grandmother to our daughters,
Katherine and Courtney.

Because of her faithful obedience,
we have known God's ideal—
a woman beautiful in His eyes.

ↄ—

We rise up and bless her!
Proverbs 31:28

Contents

An Invitation to Beauty

I have a real love for the book of Proverbs in the Bible...because that's where I first met "the Proverbs 31 woman" (Proverbs 31:10-31). She's the incredible woman who models for all women—young or seasoned, married or single—all that is beautiful in God's eyes.

Since first discovering the treasure of the Proverbs 31 woman, I've tried to model my life after her. I have sought and prayed to duplicate her actions and attitudes in developing strength of character and pursuing the responsibilities, opportunities, and dreams God gives me. And I have tried to follow after her wisdom in creating a home-sweet-home, nurturing my marriage, and raising my children.

And you'll fall in love with her too! In this remarkable woman you will find instruction, encouragement, a model to follow, and the motivation to keep you looking to God for a lifetime. And most important of all, you'll find out about true beauty—God's kind of beauty!

I'm glad you're joining me in scaling the heights of this godly beauty. God's excellent woman is someone we can follow without hesitation. And, my friend, you will never be the same after moving verse by verse through Proverbs 31:10-31! You'll grow personally and spiritually as you discover what God considers beautiful—and then apply it to your life. To help you, I've included practical *How-To's of Beauty* in each chapter. And, for even greater progress (for you or your study group), I

7

recommend the book *Beautiful in God's Eyes Growth and Study Guide*.

You and I cannot be who God wants us to be on our own power, so each chapter ends with *An Invitation to Beauty* reflective section. This "look in the mirror" gives you an opportunity to gaze into God's eyes, search your heart, and seek God's beautiful will for your life.

My heartfelt prayer as we begin, dear friend, is that you will...

- let God use this teaching about His kind of beauty to transform your heart and your life.

- share this picture of beauty from the Bible with your daughters and anyone else who is interested in God's brand of beauty.

- truly desire to become like the woman of Proverbs 31—a woman who is beautiful in God's eyes!

May it be said of you, "Many daughters have done well, but you excel them all" (Proverbs 31:29)!

In God's beautiful love,

Elizabeth George

-1-

A Rare Treasure
HER CHARACTER

⌒

"Who can find a virtuous woman?"
Proverbs 31:10 (KJV)

*H*ave you ever felt overwhelmed by a larger-than-life challenge you suddenly found yourself facing? Well, I experienced such a moment as our tour bus drove into the hotel parking lot at the base of the massive natural fortress called Masada. Jutting straight up from the shore of the Dead Sea, these fortifications built by Herod the Great towered some 1300 feet above us. It was already casting its dark and foreboding shadow over our group as the guide told us to get a good night's rest to fortify ourselves for the 7:00 A.M. climb up this ancient wonder the next day.

I felt as if I were standing at the base of Mount Everest! "What am I doing here?" I wondered. "How did this happen? I'm just a submissive wife who came to the Holy Land with her husband to study the *Bible*! I never bargained for *this*!" But now I was expected to climb up this steep mountain with the rest of the (much younger) group!

And, my new friend, I want to quickly admit that I have all these same feelings again as you and I stand at the beginning of this book about being beautiful in God's eyes, looking

9

up at *her*—the beautiful (and successful and wonderful and perfect) woman of Proverbs 31. She certainly appears to be larger than life. She's "up there," so far away, so far removed, so beautiful, so superior, so impossible. Or so it seems. . . .

But wait! Let me finish my story about Masada. I dutifully ate a healthy dinner and went to bed early, just as the guide had instructed. But I also worried all night long—Should I eat or not eat before such a strenuous climb? Should I wear jeans or shorts? How much water should I carry? . . . On and on my thoughts and fears churned. I definitely didn't get the prescribed good night's sleep!

Finally it was 6:30 in the morning—time to act. I threw on my clothes (shorts because of the brutal heat), grabbed the largest water bottle (I skipped breakfast), opened the door of our room, walked to the footpath—and I climbed Masada! I didn't want to, but I did it. It wasn't easy, and I stopped for many rests—many, *many* rests! My lungs hurt, and my legs hurt. People passed me by as I struggled. But I made it! By tapping into the deepest resources of both my mental and physical strength and by continuing to put one foot in front of the other—by taking one step after one step after one step—I finally arrived at the top of the world! (I only discovered later that the "top of the world" was sea level!) I had done what had seemed impossible—and that accomplishment was glorious!

Now, dear fellow climber, you and I face the rather daunting Proverbs 31 woman! Perhaps just as I struggled with a lack of desire to climb a mountain, you've struggled to even *want* to be like her. Maybe you've tossed and turned as you've counted the cost of such an endeavor, sensing that it will require much from you. And possibly you've suffered as other women have passed you by in their efforts to become more like her.

Whatever you're feeling, whatever your past experiences with the challenge of Proverbs 31, I invite you to come along with me now. Let's hold hands if we need to as, accepting God's invitation to become beautiful in His eyes, we climb together. Along the way we're going to tap into the grace of God's power and the Spirit-driven resolve to become all God wants us to be—and we're going to take one step at a time. After all, the Proverbs 31 woman *is* the "virtuous woman" (Proverbs 31:10), and by mastering one virtue at a time, one verse at a time, you and I are going to fully grasp her rare beauty and, by God's grace, realize it for ourselves. Pray with me now and ask God to guard you from scorning the height of His standard, from discounting this woman's superior beauty, from downplaying her virtues, or from writing her off as old-fashioned or impossible. May God's desire for you be your desire for yourself!

An Alphabet of Character

But where, you might wonder, did this woman come from? How did the woman of Proverbs 31 become a standard for godly beauty? Believe it or not, she began with a real flesh-and-blood woman!

Once upon a time there was a young prince who would someday be king, but he had many lessons to learn before then. So his mother sat down with him beside the hearth at home and taught him not only how to be a godly king but also how to find an outstanding wife.

Most scholars agree that Proverbs 31 reflects that wise mother's instruction to her young son. Verse 1 says, "The words of King Lemuel, the utterance which his mother taught him." In verses 1-9 she covers the basics of leadership, and then she describes in verses 10-31 the kind of wife he should seek, one who is indeed a rare treasure. Perhaps due to her son's young age, this wise mother organizes the list of qualities he is to look for in a wife according to the letters of the Hebrew alphabet. Taught this way, this alphabet of character could be quickly learned, easily memorized, regularly recited, and permanently etched into the tablet of his young heart (Proverbs 3:3). When the mother reached the last letter of the alphabet and finished extolling the qualities of a virtuous woman, this ode of praise became for that young prince—and for us—God's alphabet of feminine character.

As you and I begin learning the alphabet, I want us to remember two words of hope. First of all, Proverbs 31 was spoken by a woman. These are not the words or instructions of a man expressing some personal and unrealistic fantasy. True, a man (King Lemuel) is writing to us, but he is repeating a *woman's* opinion of what a woman should be! This fact inspires and encourages me. I appreciate this kind of woman-to-woman instruction as I learn more about what God finds beautiful. I want to understand the makeup of true godly beauty, and who better to show me that beauty than a beautiful-in-God's-eyes woman?

Second, even though this mother begins her alphabet with a question—"Who can find a virtuous woman?" (Proverbs 31:10)—she fully expects her son to find such a woman of character. In fact, in ancient Jerusalem, when a man married, others inquired, "Has he found a virtuous woman?"[1] Knowing such a woman is out there (verse 29), she encourages her son to look for her. The mother's faith that such a woman exists encourages me. You see, the Proverbs 31 woman is real! And you and I can be this woman—not just admire her, but *be* her! She may seem untouchable, an ideal we can't possibly attain, but she isn't. In fact, God takes great care to show her to us at other places in the Bible: He points us to Ruth, who was "a virtuous woman" (Ruth 3:11); He tells us that "a virtuous woman is [note present tense] a crown to her husband" (Proverbs 12:4 KJV); and He states that "*many* daughters have done virtuously" (Proverbs 31:29 KJV). Many!

Yes, the virtuous woman is a rare treasure—a distinctive, exceptional, extraordinary, superlative treasure—but according to God, the Author of all beauty, you and I can become all that she is. You and I can become beautiful in His eyes.

A Picture of Beauty

Since *Beautiful in God's Eyes* is the title of this book, let me clarify before we go any farther that God's idea of beauty is probably quite different from what you and I consider beautiful. (His idea of beauty is certainly far different from the world's!) So, as you read, keep in mind that Proverbs 31:10-31 presents a picture of God's idea of beauty, and—as God says about Himself—"My thoughts are not your thoughts, nor are your ways My ways. . . . My ways [are] higher than your ways, and My thoughts than your thoughts" (Isaiah 55:8-9). Just as God is in a category of His own, so is His idea of beauty!

Understanding God's kind of beauty was Step One for the young prince, and it's Step One for you and me as well. (Remember Masada? It's climbed one step at a time!) So first we have to grasp the meaning of the word *virtuous*: "Who can find a virtuous woman?" (Proverbs 31:10). The meaning of the word *virtuous* can be likened to the two sides of a coin. *Power of mind* (moral principles and attitudes) makes up the image on one side, and *power of body* (potency and effectiveness) makes up the other. Neither of these powerful traits seems to be very beautiful, but consider how God addresses them in His Proverbs 31 picture of beauty.

A *powerful mind*—In God's picture of His beautiful woman, He shows her mental strength in a composite of the internal qualities that keep her (and that will keep us) from giving up, giving in, dropping out, or quitting short of the goal to be and do what God desires. Right now look at the Proverbs 31:10-31 picture from afar. We'll take a closer look at each characteristic as we move through this book and up our mountain! God's beautiful woman is

- Pure—She is a woman of virtue (Proverbs 31:10).
- Honest—Her husband trusts her (verses 11-12).
- Industrious—She is busy from sunup to sundown managing her interests and expanding her enterprises (verses 13-19, 21-22, 24, 27, 31).
- Thrifty—Her skill with finances enables her to care for her loved ones and increase her property (verses 14, 16).
- Strong in character—She faces the daily challenges of life (and death!) with undaunted courage (verse 25, 29).
- Kind—Compassion for the unfortunate governs her life and sweet speech flows from her lips (verses 20, 26).
- Wise—Walking in wisdom is her way of life (verse 26).
- Holy—She wholeheartedly loves the Lord (verse 30).

These internal qualities enable God's beautiful woman to manage well her life, her time, her money, her mouth, her home, her relationships, and her self.

A powerful body—And how, we wonder, does the Proverbs 31 woman *do* all that God desires of her? When we turn over the "coin of definition" we clearly see that her life requires physical energy and vigor. Observe the beautiful— and strong—Proverbs 31 woman at work.

- She works willingly with her hands (Proverbs 31:13).
- Those willing hands plant a vineyard (verse 16).

- They also operate a spindle and distaff (verse 19).

- She works from early in the morning (verse 15) until late at night (verse 18).

- She nurses the needy (verse 20).

- She weaves the cloth for her family's clothes (verse 21), for her household needs (verse 22), for her own clothing (verse 22), and for sale as a professional (verse 24).

- Never idle, she watches over and builds her home (verse 27).

This virtuous and very industrious woman needs physical strength and ability to do the work of her life, the work of love.

An Army of Virtues

And now, dear reader, having considered this special woman's moral and physical strength, we must look at one final element that is crucial to understanding what a virtuous woman is. I know it doesn't sound very attractive or feminine or beautiful, but she is an army—an army of virtues! That's the essence of God's description of her character. Let me explain.

The Hebrew word for *virtuous* is used 200-plus times in the Bible to describe an army. This Old Testament word refers to *a force* and is used to mean *able, capable, mighty, strong, valiant, powerful, efficient, wealthy,* and *worthy*.[2] The word is also used in reference to a man of war, men of war, and men prepared for war. Change this definition to the feminine case and you begin to grasp the power at the core of this woman! Just as mental toughness and physical energy are the primary traits of an army, they also mark God's beautiful woman.

I know this is a lot to absorb, so you may want to go back and read this important section again. As you and I stand together staring at the awesome Proverbs 31 woman, we need to understand as much as possible what God means when He describes her as a virtuous woman. After all, understanding her character—the goal of this chapter—is our first step toward becoming virtuous Proverbs 31 women ourselves!

"Who can find a virtuous woman?" is the question of Proverbs 31:10. With this query God points out that His kind of woman is extraordinary—indeed, a rare treasure—when it comes to her inner strength and outward accomplishments. She's also an utterly awesome army of virtues. And with God's help you and I can become awesome, too! Here are some initial steps.

The How-To's of Beauty

1. Cultivate the desire—Based on Moses' prayer in Psalm 90:10 ("The days of our lives are seventy years; and if by reason of strength they are eighty years"), imagine yourself sitting back and enjoying your eightieth birthday! A host of people has gathered to celebrate with you at this special party in your honor. Suddenly a fanfare announces the arrival of your birthday cake. As it's wheeled in, you marvel at how big it is! It has to be because it has 80 candles on it, and every one of them is lighted. In fact, the heat from their blaze makes you wish you hadn't worn a sweater!

Now for the challenge: If the Lord allows you to live to enjoy such a birthday party, what do you want to have accomplished by the time you blow out the candles that represent 80 years of life?

My friend, I'm praying right now that your answer to this crucial question will indicate your heartfelt desire to be a woman of character, a woman who is beautiful in God's eyes!

2. Give it time—How did God's beautiful woman become such a rare, exceptional, extraordinary treasure, such a woman of strong godly character? In a word, it took *time*! Nothing this grand happens overnight; nothing this grand just happens!

What kind of time does the development of virtuous character require?

Time reading God's Word—Make daily time for reading God's Word your highest priority. Maybe this story will help you understand why reading the Bible cultivates beauty. When I was in Israel, a foremost exporter of diamonds, I learned that one step in the process of diamond production is polishing the gem. A diamond is never released to the marketplace until the person assigned to polish it can see the image of his own face reflected in the jewel.

Well, dear one, you are a diamond in the rough, and you gain the power of character—you begin to more clearly reflect your heavenly Father's face—as His Holy Word smoothes and polishes your character. As you spend time gazing into God's Word, the light of His truth brightens your motivation to live your life for His glory. When you read the Word of the Lord, He uses it to scrub and scour away your fears, your laziness, your doubts, and your sinful ways. God uses His Word to transform you into a woman of divine power who more brilliantly reflects His beauty.

Time memorizing God's Word—Besides reading God's Word daily, set up a plan for regularly memorizing Scripture. My plan involves working on Scripture while I take my daily walk. Sure, the exercise contributes to my physical power (and even my physical beauty as it keeps the pounds off!), but the Scripture verses I memorize *while* I am walking give me the mental and spiritual force I need to "climb" toward God's kind of beauty—for one more day.

Time with other women—Surround yourself with women who encourage your spiritual growth (Titus 2:3). I know from experience there's nothing like relationships with sisters in Christ. God has blessed me with my "faithful five," five women who are endeavoring to spend the 80 years of their lives (Lord willing!) becoming God's beautiful women. We are committed to loving, encouraging, and praying for one another along the way. Fellowship with these women who delight in living for God spurs me on in my heart's desire to be a beautiful woman of character.

Time reading biographies of God's saints—Begin a reading program—even for five minutes a day. I've found that time spent getting to know the great saints of the faith is time well spent. Being touched by the lives of God's "army" of women gives me a fresh infusion of strength as I consider their physical strength and their mental endurance.

- Amy Carmichael was a missionary to India who never took a furlough from ministry in her 55 years of serving.

- Susanna Wesley was a mother of 19 children (ten of whom died before the age of two) who taught and raised her children (including John and Charles Wesley, the founders of the Methodist movement) at the same time that she managed the family farm during her husband's imprisonment and endured religious persecution from her neighbors.

- Elisabeth Elliot served as a jungle missionary, suffered the loss of one husband by martyrdom and another to a lingering cancer, and raised her daughter as a single mom.

- Edith Schaeffer forsook a life of comfort to forge a new ministry with her husband Francis in Europe. At L'Abri, she suffered from local persecution, terrifying avalanches, a lack of medical care for a child with polio and another with a rheumatic heart condition, and later the death of her husband after a five-year struggle with cancer.

- Ruth Graham faithfully looked after five children while their father and her husband Billy served the Lord away from home for many months each year.

On and on the list of God's beautiful women goes—and you and I can draw enormous strength from their example.

Time today—Dedicate the remainder of your day (and your tomorrows) to God and live it His way. "As now, so then," one wise saying instructs. It's true that if we want to be God's beautiful woman at that eightieth birthday party—or at any other time—we have to be her today! After all, today is what our tomorrows are made of. That truth is behind Moses' plea for God to "teach us to number our days that we may gain a heart of wisdom" (Psalm 90:12). You see, as we try to live our life today as God wants us to live it, and as we cultivate the character qualities He says are beautiful, then we will be beautiful and wise today—and, in God's hands, the tomorrows will take care of themselves.

Time over a lifetime—You and I don't ever need to be discouraged or feel overwhelmed by God's standard for beauty because He gives us, day by day, a lifetime to reach it. Hear what beautiful and wise Edith Schaeffer says about the Proverbs 31 woman: "Certainly all the admirable things written about this woman did not take place in one year. It seems to me it is a summary of the great diversity of accomplishments and results of her work and imagination and talents over a long period of time."[3]

An Invitation to Beauty

Whew! I feel as if I've already climbed a mountain by just trying to describe God's beautiful woman. Maybe you do, too, after trying to absorb the richness of her portrait.

I'm also feeling somewhat tentative (do I really want this?), fearful (what if I fail?), and sober (it will be a hard climb!). And at moments I even wonder, "What difference will it make if I try to live such a virtuous life?" But that kind of thinking ends when you and I remember that the description of this special woman is in God's Word: she is *God's* portrait, and she reflects *God's* idea of beauty and *God's* design for excellence. *He* knows the value of the work He has given us to do for Him and what it takes mentally and physically to accomplish it. Perhaps we are beginning to realize why this woman of strength is "a rare treasure"!

Why not join me in whispering a plea to God for strength—*His* strength? Why not declare with me your desire to become a woman who, like an army, moves through the challenges and duties of life with valor, courage, bravery, stamina, endurance, and power—*His* power? I know you want the same thing I want—to truly be a woman who is beautiful in God's eyes, to enjoy His approval, His "well done, good and faithful servant" (Matthew 25:21), His acknowledgment that "*you* are a virtuous woman" (Ruth 3:11)!

-2-

A Sparkling Jewel
HER VALUE

∽

"Her price is much higher than jewels."[1]
Proverbs 31:10

*I*t was a dream come true! I was finally going to meet her! I'm talking about the Proverbs 31 woman, the woman who is beautiful in God's eyes, the woman we'll be getting to know throughout this book. My husband Jim was taking students from The Master's Seminary to Israel for some intensive study, and he invited me to come along!

You see, he knew. He knew that for 25 years I had done everything I could to learn about this beautiful woman. He knew I had memorized many versions of Proverbs 31:10-31. He also knew (from our checkbook!) that I had made her exemplary life a special study project for that same quarter-century, investing in a library of books about the Proverbs and about her. And he knew the pursuit of her exemplary lifestyle was a personal lifetime goal of mine. Yes, Jim definitely knew what meeting her would mean to me. As I said, a trip to her homeland to meet the Proverbs 31 woman was a dream come true!

So I did what many women do before a trip—I made lists! Of course the list of things that had to be done before I could leave home and office for a month was long. The packing list was long, too, and so was the shopping list of items to pick up before we departed. But I carefully—and prayerfully—created another list before we left, a list so personal and so important that I carried it in my Bible during the entire trip. I titled it "Things to See" and noted every cultural aspect from Proverbs 31:10-31 that I wanted to see for myself in Israel. I was on a mission. "Who can find a virtuous woman?" Proverbs 31:10 asks. Well, I was going to find her!

The first item on my "must see" list was *jewels*. I wrote this down because Proverbs 31:10 (the verse this chapter is about) begins with a statement about the value of her character: "Her price is much higher than jewels." I wanted to see firsthand the jewels in the land of Israel that reflect the value of God's beautiful woman so I could take another step toward understanding her better and appreciating her more.

Searching for Treasure

You and I began our search for God's beautiful woman in chapter 1 as we listened in on a mother teaching a class of one—her young son—about true feminine beauty. Her lesson stressed what an extraordinary and exceptional treasure a truly godly woman is. And now as we read on, we see that the mother reiterates the woman's value by referring to jewels: "Her price is much higher than jewels" (Proverbs 31:10).

- "Her worth is far above rubies," one translator tells us.[2] The rich red ruby is truly a unique gem, and because of their rarity, large rubies even surpass diamonds of equal weight in value![3]

- "Her value is far beyond pearls," another translation states.[4] Consider that only twenty pearls are found in 35,000 pearl oysters—and only three of those are gem quality![5]

- "Far beyond corals is her worth," still another reading of the Bible declares.[6] Corals are delicate "flower-animals," and only a few are quality enough to be polished and regarded as precious stones.[7]

Rubies. Pearls. Corals. Take your pick. Each of these sparkling jewels is quite rare *and* valuable. Each is hard to harvest and few are found. And that's the imagery our young prince's mother uses to impress upon him how extraordinary a woman who is beautiful—in God's eyes—would be. Once found, she would be of inestimable value!

Now let me tell you, my beautiful friend, what I found on my personal treasure-hunt in Israel. As I told you, my list of "Things to See" had jewels right at the top. So, when our study group spent a day in the Israel Museum, I dashed in and began searching for jewels. On and on the museum's displays went, and on and on my search continued. Covering every hall, I found not a single jewel! The jewels—along with every other item of value—had been carried away by conquering armies in days gone by.

But what I did find in the museum was as telling as what I didn't find. You see, the Israel Museum is filled with artifacts that have been unearthed in that country, and these artifacts represent the nation's rich and long history. What were some of the relics that give us clues into the life lived by God's beautiful woman? I feasted my eyes on . . . bones and coffins! Walls were covered with shields and swords, body armor and instruments of war! Cases displayed dishes and cookware made out of mud! Stone olive presses and millstones for grinding grains were also on display. These were not at all what I had expected!

What lesson did such primitive items offer? They were a voice which spoke of hard times—of struggling to survive, of eking out a living, of barely managing to exist. These items spoke of work and war, labor and loss. There was little—if any—beauty, color, or evidence of pleasure. Everything I saw was stark, bleak, and basic, testifying to a life that was stark, bleak, and basic.

Then it hit me! I suddenly realized that God's beautiful Proverbs 31 woman was the sparkling jewel in her husband's life! She brought the love, the color, the joy, the life, and the energy to the home. Yes, life was bleak in Israel, and everyday life focused on just surviving in that dry, rugged land. Food, clothing, and shelter were all-consuming daily concerns. But, with a wife who was a sparkling jewel, a man would find life bearable. In fact, with God's beautiful woman beside him, he possessed treasure untold!

The How-To's of Beauty

I said God's truth hit me—and it hit me hard! Emotionally I staggered as I realized the magnitude of God's plan for me (and for you, too!): I am to supply beauty in the lives of my husband and children as we struggle through life together. I am to light up the home with sparkle no matter how hard times are.

I hope you are catching a vision of your life as a sparkling jewel to those who face hardship, pain, weariness, drudgery, or sorrow. Being a jewel in the lives of those He blesses us with is a tall order from God, but He knows you and I can—by His beautiful grace—fill it!

Just as gems increase in value as time passes, we who are God's beautiful women—His jewels—should, too. So here are some exercises to help us enhance our sparkle and brighten up our life as well as the lives of those around us.

1. *Grow in practical skills*—Married or single, we who are God's women need to sharpen the skills necessary for managing a home (or apartment or dorm room).

Homemaking—I well remember the sad tears of a college graduate about to marry whose mother had financed swimming lessons, encouraged her athletic efforts, and driven her to swimming pools, swim practice, and swim meets for 20 years. My friend could swim—but she couldn't cook or clean! Another woman had the same problem. Actually I should say her *husband* had the problem. One day he showed up in Jim's office at The Master's Seminary. You see, he went home every evening after his classes and his job to— nothing! Nothing was cooked, nothing was cooking, nothing was in the cupboard or refrigerator *to* cook, and his wife also had nothing of a plan for what to cook in mind. She was clueless! And he was helpless—and hungry!

Money management—God's beautiful women also need a working knowledge of personal finances. We need to know about paying bills, managing a checkbook, reconciling a bank statement, nurturing savings and investments, and holding the reins on those charge cards. Jim says that one of my greatest gifts to him has been taking care of our family finances. By managing his paycheck I've given him back hours of time every week for 30-plus years, hours he can spend on other responsibilities at home, at work, and at church. As you and I work our way through Proverbs 31:10- 31, you'll notice again and again the keen business head on God's beautiful woman!

Time management—Diligent time management is key to running a home (and a life!) smoothly. Time is the most precious commodity God gives us, and He expects it to be redeemed (Colossians 4:5) and used for His purposes (Ephesians 2:10). Life itself is made up of minutes, and those minutes must be managed wisely and well. I encourage you to begin the daily habit of planning and scheduling. If you don't know how to begin, invest in some time management books or talk with the women you know who excel in this practical skill.

2. *Grow in emotional stability*—Certainly to be a sparkling jewel in anyone's life, you and I need to be growing in emotional stability. After all, the mistress of the home determines the general emotional atmosphere under her roof; her emotional state sets the standard and the tone. Proverbs speaks numerous times of the shrewish woman who is rottenness to her husband's bones (Proverbs 12:4) and the brawling woman whose husband can no longer endure living in the same house with her (21:9 and 19; 25:24). I know neither you nor I want to be this kind of unattractive woman. Our desire is to live out an epitaph found on a gravestone. The husband of 60 years said of his wife that "she always made home happy." What a wonderful tribute to his sparkling jewel!

Since this book is about becoming a virtuous woman—a woman of mental, emotional, physical, and spiritual strength—here are three guidelines for gaining some emotional stability so that you, too, can make your home happy.

Master your tolerance—By this I mean your endurance. Emotional stability gives every soldier in every army the invaluable ability to continue on when the going is tough, and that's what I'm calling you to do. I'm calling you to learn endurance, something I've been working towards for decades. Ever since I discovered that God's beautiful and virtuous woman is an army of virtues, I've been trying to learn a soldier's ability to persevere, and I turn to God to be my Helper.

When I face difficult circumstances or painful times, I pray something like this: "God, Your Word says You have already given me all things that pertain to life and godliness

(2 Peter 1:3). And Your Word says I can do all things—including handle this—through Christ who strengthens me (Philippians 4:13). By Your grace and through Your Spirit, I can do this. Thank You for enabling me to meet the challenge!"

With this prayer I acknowledge the marvelous resources I have in the Lord and then bear down physically and mentally like a soldier and march right through what lies before me. I endeavor to quietly . . . and calmly . . . and determinedly . . . endure life's challenges as they roll in and out with the regularity of the ocean's surf. You see, my goal—my prayer—is always that I will not give in, give up, or quit. Instead of becoming incapacitated by emotions, I want to be that soldier who is beautiful in God's eyes, and I know you join me in that desire.

Master your temper—I'm using *temper* to refer to "heat of mind" (as *Webster's* says) and passion. When it comes to temper, God's Word tells us a few things about a woman of strength.

- She nurtures a peaceful heart (Proverbs 14:30).
- She knows how to wait (Proverbs 19:2).
- She does not strive (Proverbs 19:11).
- She restrains her spirit (Proverbs 25:28).

This description may seem like another impossible dream, but let me reassure you that God uses our faithful devotion to Him and our careful attention to His standards day by day, incident by incident, challenge by challenge over a lifetime to flesh out in us His divine beauty, a reflection of His image.

I started down this path of mastering my temper by first creating a "resolutions" page in my personal prayer notebook.

This list (you can tell I'm a list-maker!) contained the deadly sins I was holding up to God daily with a heart-plea for Him to help me eliminate them out of my life (Matthew 5:29-30). One such unbeautiful habit on that list read, "Stop screaming at the children." I hope you get the picture!

Master your tongue—Speaking of deadly sins, don't most of them involve the tongue? Blessing and cursing do indeed proceed out of the same mouth (James 3:10). Our words can either "speak like the piercings of a sword" or "promote health" (Proverbs 12:18). To bring the sparkle of God's beauty into a home, you and I need to live out a few more wise proverbs. Specifically, we need to:

- Speak less often (Proverbs 10:19).
- Speak only after we think about what we're going to say (Proverbs 15:28).
- Speak only what is sweet and pleasant (Proverbs 16:21 and 24).
- Speak only what is wise and kind (Proverbs 31:26).

In light of this topic, I can't resist passing on to you one of our family's all-time favorite devotionals from the *Our Daily Bread* series. The morning Jim read it at the breakfast table, my daughter Katherine drew five stars and wrote the word "Mom" on it. That day was May 17, 1982—a red-letter day for our family. Maybe this will help you, too.

A woman developed a very serious throat condition. The doctor prescribed medication but told her that her vocal cords needed total rest—no talking for six months! With a husband and six children to care for, it seemed an impossible order, but she cooperated. When she needed the youngsters, she blew a whistle. Instructions became written memos, and questions were answered on pads of paper she had placed around the house. The six months passed, and after she recovered, her first comments were quite revealing. She said that the children had become quieter, and then remarked, "I don't think I'll ever holler again like I used to." When asked about the notes, she replied, "You'd be surprised how many, written hastily, I crumpled up and threw into the wastebasket before I gave them to anyone to read. Seeing my words before anyone heard them had an effect that I don't think I can ever forget."[8]

I got the message: Speak less often . . . and only after thinking about what I'm going to say. And speak only what is sweet and pleasant . . . only what is wise and kind! These are God's guidelines for beautiful speech.

An Invitation to Beauty

Don't you want God's kind of practical beauty and inner strength in your life, too, dear sister? Don't you deeply desire to be beautiful in His eyes, to be a blazing jewel who adds sparkle to the lives of others?

We must pay a price if we are to become priceless, if we are to become women whose "price is much higher than jewels." Such rare beauty of character is hard-won as is the beauty of the jewels we so prize. Gems are hard to begin with, and these rough, hard gems need to be cut. All the flaws, all that is unlovely about them, need to be removed. Once cut, these gems are polished to add to their luster and increase their brilliance, to allow color to shine through, and to create its "fire," a rainbow-like sparkle. Our sparkle comes by such a process, too, as—married or single—we gain greater emotional stability and sharpen our practical skills. With these two core elements inside, we who long to be God's beautiful gems will indeed sparkle.

Oh, dear one, God, our Master Craftsman, is holding your heart (and mine) in His hands. Will you look into His eyes, see His love for you, and choose to let Him do His purifying work? Will you yield to Him the flaws in your life that inhibit your "fire," your sparkle? Will you ask Him to help you not succumb to any harmful emotions? And will you do your part to grow in emotional stability and to polish your skills? These two traits—your character and the skills that reflect that character—are so desirable to Him and so valuable to others. Let God work His beauty process in you!

And now, on to a closer look at another sparkling feature of the woman who is beautiful in God's eyes.

-3-

A Solid Rock
HER LOYALTY

ↄ‿

"The heart of her husband safely trusts her."
Proverbs 31:11

I once read about a couple who exchanged their wedding vows on top of the Rock of Gibraltar, the famed rock island at the entrance to the Mediterranean Sea. The groom explained that they wanted to found their marriage on a rock. Well, far better for a husband than saying one's vows on the Rock of Gibraltar is establishing a marriage on the rock of Jesus Christ and the bedrock loyalty of his wife! When a man marries a woman who is mentally, emotionally, physically, and spiritually strong, he can confidently build his life, his work, and his home, trusting in her rock-solid character to be a cornerstone for his efforts.

Believe me, after studying in Israel and living in Jerusalem for three weeks, I know a lot about rocks! Climbing through the hill country day after day meant taking on the characteristics of a gazelle as we walked up, over, around, between, and back down the rocks. And the tells we visited—those layers of remains from Old Testament cities—consisted of layers upon layers of rock and stone, all resting on a foundation of bedrock.

But, the most exciting rock I saw was a cornerstone. I took a picture of it (in fact, I'm looking at it as I write) because God speaks of His women as "cornerstones" (Psalm 144:12 KJV). I chose the cornerstone at the excavated base of the south end of the Temple Mount, the site of Herod's Temple (where Jesus worshiped). Supporting the massive foundation of the Temple, this ancient cornerstone has sustained the weight of 75-foot-high stone walls for more than 2,000 years. Twenty feet long, the standard height-of-a-man high (six feet), and at least eight feet across, it still holds the weight of the entire Temple wall.

This remarkable cornerstone had been carefully selected because Herod wanted a firm foundation for the wonder he was building. This most important building had to be stable, so Herod chose a rock that was more than adequate enough to be the cornerstone. Definitely a solid rock, it has not budged despite 2,000 years of battles, earthquakes, elements, and the erosion of time—and neither has the wall on top of it!

Like that wall, your marriage can be strengthened as you, my sister in the Lord, become—by His grace—a virtuous woman of strength who stands steady as a rock. The cornerstone I have a picture of may not be beautiful and most of it is buried and out of sight, but Herod's Temple was splendid! I want you to carry this image of a cornerstone with you through this chapter because the picture of a wife standing as steady and strong as a rock is at the heart of Proverbs 31:11.

The Language of Loyalty

I thought I knew all about trust, but I have to admit I found three surprises as I studied the statement "the heart of her husband safely trusts her" (Proverbs 31:11). These surprises taught me even more about the importance of being a rock to my husband Jim.

Rest—First consider "the *heart* of her husband." The Hebrew word for *heart* actually refers to the mind where doubt, anxiety, and restlessness fester. But the heart (the mind) of a husband who can trust a loyal wife is a heart at ease, a heart at rest. Our calling as God's women is to live life in such a solid way that our husband never worries or wonders about our character or our management of our home, our finances, or our time! Then he can truly build his life on the cornerstone of our loyalty, his heart resting in—and on—the steady support of his wife.

Encouragement—Next comes the trust factor: "The heart of her husband safely *trusts* her." The Hebrew word for *trust* translates "to be of good courage, to take heart and to feel confidence."[1] Therefore, a man married to one of God's beautiful women feels confident—he is encouraged—by his ability to trust in his wife![2] Her loyalty is a daily ministry of encouragement to him. Because of his confidence in her (he "safely trusts *her*"), he is encouraged and strengthened for his tasks.

Trust in God—Throughout the book of Proverbs trusting in any person or pursuit other than God is equated to foolishness (see Proverbs 3:5). But God makes one exception to His principle: Whereas a man usually enjoys wealth as a result of his trust in God, here in Proverbs 31:11 his profit is a result of the value of *his wife*—in whom he can solidly trust. He trusts his wife in the same way he trusts God![3] "The heart of her husband safely trusts in *her*"—and in the Lord! As one translator sees it, "The heart of her husband has faith in her"![4] Imagine, a calling to work together with God to comfort and support our mate. What an incredible privilege and ministry!

Checklist for Loyalty

These three surprises give me a lot to think about. It's staggering to realize that because of me (when I follow God's guidelines, that is), my Jim can enjoy rest, confidence, and a deeper trust in the Lord.

As I considered the impact our loyalty has on our hard-working husbands, I again skimmed Proverbs 31:10-31 and jotted down a personal checklist for loyalty. If you're not married, this is still relevant. Remember, after all, that this mother is advising her son to search for a *single* woman who *already* possesses this beautiful quality of loyalty! Any and all of God's beautiful women should be worthy of this description: faithful, true, and constant; a solid rock in terms of her character, her marriage, her family, her relationships, and her ministry. So, whether we are married or single, our goal is for this priceless virtue to become a jewel in our crown (Proverbs 12:4)!

Here's my personal checklist for loyalty in ten different spheres of daily life. Why not consider how you measure up against God's standards? Are you building your life, your home, and your marriage on these rocks?

Money—Can your husband's heart and mind rest because of your diligent management of his (and your) assets (Proverbs 31:27)? Can he depend on you to be thrifty, wise, and debt-free?

Children—Are you a devoted mother, dedicated to training up obedient children who love the Lord, who love their father, and who bring honor to their names (Proverbs 31:1-2)?

Home—Is your husband encouraged by the knowledge that all is well—and will be well—at home because of your focused efforts to run an orderly home (Proverbs 31:13,27)?

Reputation—Is your husband's heart at rest because he knows that you will do him good and not evil all the days of your life, never causing any questions about his character to arise (Proverbs 31:12,23)?

Fidelity—Can your husband trust and even rejoice in your life-long faithfulness to your wedding vows (Proverbs 5:18)?

Emotions—Does your husband rest in the knowledge that he can depend on you to be emotionally steady and stable, avoiding blow-ups and flare-ups (Proverbs 14:30)?

Happiness—Are you a fountain of joy, delighting yourself in the Lord (Psalm 37:4) and refreshing the hearts of those at home?

Wisdom—Can your husband trust you to handle the challenges, difficulties, and crises of life with godly wisdom (Proverbs 19:14)?

Conduct—Can your husband count on you to conduct yourself with graciousness (Proverbs 11:16), discretion (Proverbs 11:22), virtue (Proverbs 31:10), and dignity (Proverbs 31:25)?

Love—Positive progress in the preceding nine areas is progress in love! You see, love is known by its actions. Your active care for your husband's assets and the details of his life is powerful evidence of your love for him (Proverbs 31:29).

I hope you are beginning to appreciate how highly God values loyalty in you and me! Do you understand why loyalty is so beautiful in His eyes—and in your husband's? Here in Proverbs 31, loyalty is number one on God's list of character traits, and you (and I) can take specific, concrete steps—daily and for the rest of your life—to lay a firm foundation of loyal character and earn a greater degree of trust from everyone you meet.

The How-To's of Beauty

1. *Take trust seriously*—We need to take seriously whatever God says whenever He speaks! And God says "a virtuous woman"—a woman who's faithful, a wife who's loyal—can be trusted. The best way to begin laying this cornerstone of godly beauty is to place it at the top of your daily prayer list. Ask God to transform your character.

2. *Keep your word*—I remember listening to some college women share prayer requests at their weekly Bible study in our home. They earnestly and eagerly wanted others to pray that they would become "women of their word," women who were true to their word. That's a good goal for us, too. So challenge yourself to do what you say you'll do, be where you say you'll be, and keep the appointments you make.

3. *Follow through on instructions*—The degree to which we follow through on instructions is a measure of our faithfulness and our loyalty. In Genesis 3:1-6, for instance, we see how Eve failed her husband—and God—when she failed to follow the Lord's guidelines regarding the tree of knowledge and ate the forbidden fruit (Genesis 2:17). Her failure to follow God's directions sent the world reeling. Her sin—her desire to do things her way and not God's way—toppled a perfect creation and required the sacrifice of His only Son to bring us back into fellowship with Him (2 Corinthians 11:3; 1 Timothy 2:14).

So one way you can build trust is to do what you've been asked to do. Try not to second-guess the whys behind instructions. And don't get too creative with directions. Ask questions if you need to, but in the end your goal is to follow through. If your husband wants the paper canceled today, do it. If he needs his clothes picked up from the cleaners, do it. If he asks you to have the oil changed in the car, do it. If he's on a special diet, fix it. *His* heart can be at ease because he knows that *you* are carrying out his desires for the home, the family, and the finances. Furthermore, your compliance is evidence of God's deep character buried in your heart!

4. *When in doubt, check it out!*—One day a wife who was working on building her husband's trust in her took his car to be worked on. While the car was up on the rack, the mechanic noticed a "what-you-ma'-call-it" that needed to be replaced. When he asked her if she wanted it replaced ("So glad we caught it! You sure wouldn't want that to break while you're out driving! Won't take but a minute—and a few more dollars, of course—if we do it right now"), she was ready to blurt out an enthusiastic "Yes!" when she remembered her goal. When she called her husband to check it out, he said it was something he could easily—and cheaply—replace. And then he thanked her for calling! She could sense his grateful heart, a heart that rested because she checked with him first. Her wise actions built her husband's trust in her, served him well, and saved them money—all at the same time!

So, when in doubt, check it out. Call your husband and get his input. (P.S. Seeking counsel like this is also a mark of wisdom. Proverbs 28:26 says, "He that trusts in his own heart is a fool.")

5. *Be accountable*—When Jim and I were teaching our teenage daughters Katherine and Courtney about accountability and trustworthiness, we let them leave the house only after they let us know where they would be and agreed to check in if their plans changed.

And I do the same thing as a wife! You see, I want Jim to know where I am every minute. This goal becomes quite a challenge when I travel to speaking engagements. Jim is usually with me, but when he isn't, I phone, I fax, I e-mail, and

I leave a travel itinerary complete with all names, locations, phone numbers, fax numbers, flight numbers, and flight times. I call him from every airport—with every plane change—and from every conference site. We even have a toll-free 800 number and 50-state cell phone coverage so I can call him from Anywhere, U.S.A., without any hassle. It's very important to me that Jim knows exactly where I am. Even when I run my daily errands at home, I let him know where I am going and when I'll be back.

Your husband should know where you are at all times. Keeping him informed speaks loudly of your willingness to be accountable to him and nurtures his trust in you and your relationship. Besides—returning to Eve's story—didn't Satan deceive her (Genesis 3:1) when she was away from her husband's protection and failed to check in?

An Invitation to Beauty

And now, my loyal friend and beautiful sister, it's time to turn our hearts to the Father and look full into His wonderful face. As we discussed, whenever God speaks, we need to take His word seriously. And here in Proverbs 31:11 God states His desire that we exhibit one of His personal attributes—His faithfulness. You and I trust the Lord because we can count on His faithfulness. David, who trusted God, proclaimed, "You are my rock" (Psalm 31:3). God asks you to show forth His kind of faithfulness to your husband; He asks you to be a solid rock for your husband to trust in and lean on.

Do you want to be beautiful in God's eyes? Do you want to reflect His loyalty and faithfulness in your life? Then you need *His* marvelous grace, power, faithfulness, and strength—so that you can be dependable in all areas of life. You need to choose to be a woman of your word (and His!) and a woman who follows instructions in the details of daily life.

This chapter is entitled "A Solid Rock," and, dear one, that's exactly what you'll be for your mate (and others) as you consistently live out your loyalty to him. Life is difficult and filled with hardships, and your husband carries a heavy load of responsibility. He needs a solid rock to rest his soul upon, and you have the privilege of being that kind of rock! Will you extend to your husband the gift of a heart at rest? Will you provide him an oh-so-needed rock to rest on? Will you begin today to make the virtue of loyalty a lifetime aim as God transforms you into one of His treasured cornerstones (Psalm 144:12)?

-4-

An Unfailing Prize
HER CONTRIBUTION

ᥱ᥈

"He will have no lack of gain."
Proverbs 31:11

*H*ere's something I think you'll want to read," Jim said as he handed me the business section of our daily newspaper. (And I think you'll want to read this chapter, too!) The feature article offered the following advice for, as the title said, "Building Your Nest Egg":

- Keep track of your expenditures.
- Cut back on spending.
- Shop wisely.
- Stay out of debt (especially credit card debt).
- Save six months' worth of living expenses for emergencies.
- Set aside money each month for savings and investments.
- Invest aggressively.[1]

I had to blink! My newspaper was describing the wisdom God's beautiful woman already possesses . . . and practices! As a master in micromanagement, she's already following this advice and making an invaluable contribution to her family's financial well-being.

The Spoils of War

Along with the sterling virtues God's beautiful woman possesses, her financial contribution to her household makes her invaluable to her husband and her family. Because she herself is an unfailing prize, her husband "will have no lack of gain" (Proverbs 31:11). Let me explain.

A *military prize*—The word "gain" derives its significance from the cultural setting of Proverbs. In those days when one army defeated another, the victorious ruler and his soldiers carried off the spoils of war. These spoils were the prizes of war and comprised wealth in a time when there was no coinage.

With this verse from Proverbs 31 in mind, I stood a long time in the Israel Museum studying a 15' by 50' clay relief found on a wall in Babylon. It pictured the historic siege of the great Palestinian city of Lakish in 701 B.C. (2 Chronicles 32:9). The left side of the picture detailed the raging battle taking place at the gate and around the walls of the city. The right side showed the victors carrying off the prizes of war—people for servants, livestock for food, and treasures of silver, gold, jewels, and clothing.

A *peaceful prize*—But wealth could be acquired without facing the threat of death in battle. There were other, more peaceful ways to obtain wealth. A man could, for instance, lie, cheat, or steal; he could borrow money; he could become an indentured servant, hiring himself out for long periods of time in faraway places.

A *personal prize*—The woman who is beautiful in God's eyes, however, determines that by her personal contribution to her husband's finances "he will have no lack of gain" (verse 11). She doesn't want him to lack anything, but she also doesn't want him to be forced to leave her, his children, or his home to go off to war—to endanger his life—in order to bring home the spoils to pay off debts or increase his personal wealth. And she certainly doesn't want him to be tempted to obtain money by unrighteous means! So she chooses to give of herself—her mind, her strength—to do the work and make the necessary contribution so that her husband will "have no lack of gain." We easily see that she herself is the gain, the wealth, the unfailing prize!

The "Warrior"

She is also a warrior. We defined the word *virtuous* in chapter 1 as meaning an army, and that idea is repeated here. The Hebrew and Greek languages give us a vivid metaphoric picture of this woman, this unfailing prize, as a mighty warrior who utilizes her abilities for the benefit of her husband's domain.[2]

This startling image dramatically conveys the commitment of God's beautiful woman to her husband and his wealth and welfare. She is a warrior of undying allegiance who dedicates her life and energies to the well-being of her husband and his household. *She* battles daily on the home front so that *he* doesn't have to engage in war or experience a "lack of gain"!

The Beauty of God's Plan

I know this may sound crass, unspiritual, and quite unbeautiful, but much of Proverbs 31:10-31 deals with money. God's 22-verse portrait of His beautiful woman clearly shows her daily involvement in managing, making, and multiplying money. When I read this, I wondered why money management is so important in God's eyes, and learning why was a good exercise for me. Here are some of the reasons money matters to God.

God is honored—This teaching from Proverbs 31 about family finance—about making, managing, and multiplying money—is God's design for His beautiful women. He is honored when we follow His plan.

Your husband is blessed—Money management is a ministry to your husband which gives him relief of mind *and* release of time. Even if your husband oversees finances in a general way, you are the one who runs the home and therefore manages the money on a day-to-day basis. You can, for instance, manage the food budget, save money by using coupons, shop wisely, and cook instead of buying prepared foods or eating out.

Your children benefit—As your children see firsthand how you, a mother who is beautiful in God's eyes, handle money, they will be greatly blessed. They will learn many lessons as they watch you manage money, make money, save money, and give money away (children notice our faithful giving at church!). Your children will develop a healthy respect for money, an appreciation of stewardship, an ability to be disciplined with finances, and personal savings goals and money management skills of their own. You will be training them for life by your example.

Your home is built—The Proverbs teach that "every wise woman builds her house" (Proverbs 14:1) and "through wisdom a house is built" (Proverbs 24:3). What characterizes the house wisdom builds? "The rooms are filled with all precious and pleasant riches" (Proverbs 24:4). How can you build such a home? By keen oversight of the finances. Yours will be a house of plenty—truly a home-sweet-home!

Your character grows—Proverbs 31 clearly shows that, in God's eyes, wise money management is a virtue. And God calls us to nurture the sister virtue of self-control in the area of money. Usually the one person you have to especially watch if you're going to save money is *yourself*! After all, every decision *not* to spend money is money saved! When you learn to do without, when you learn to say no, you reap great rewards: The savings grow, the expenses fall, and the bank account builds—all of which motivates you to continue your wise money management!

A Personal Story

In the early days of our marriage, Jim handled our finances. He paid the bills, balanced the checkbook, and kept our files and records. But as his life became more complicated, money management became more burdensome. I didn't like seeing him stay up late at night, hunched over the checkbook, and I hated those mornings when he had to dash off last-minute checks before he headed out the door. I dreaded the days of paperwork he faced before and after his long missions trips. And I dared not look at what was lying in those piles of paperwork I dutifully dusted around on his desk! Our lives were marked by mad scrambling to get to the post office, waiting in line the "day-of" to make on-time payments, and the frustration of finance charges, late fees, and overdraft penalties.

Memorizing Proverbs 31:10-31 and studying the life of God's beautiful woman helped me realize that I could ease Jim's life by taking over some of this responsibility for him. Under his tutelage I learned the basics of bookkeeping, bill paying, and banking, and I began contributing to our financial well-being. No, I didn't have a job or bring in a paycheck at the time, but let me tell you some of the ways I did contribute financially—and still do today.

- I paid all bills on time, saving on finance charges and late fees. That meant money in the bank.

- We opened a savings account and signed up to have some money automatically withdrawn from each of Jim's paychecks and deposited into that account. That meant fewer trips to the bank, less paperwork, and more savings.

- We reconcile all bank statements the day we receive them. That means that we know our current financial condition. It also means no bounced checks and therefore more money in the bank.

- The checkbook shows an up-to-the-minute balance, signaling to us exactly where we stand every day of the month. That means savings realized by not overspending.

Needless to say, Jim was greatly relieved when I started to contribute to our financial health and strength in these ways. The time my labor redeemed for him was spent in other productive ways around the house and in ministry. Our evenings took on a lighter tone, and our mornings were more relaxed. We experienced a wonderful sense of freedom as we gained control of our finances.

But my contribution didn't end with the four steps outlined above. They were only the beginning! I took flight and began reading to learn better money management skills, principles, and methods. This led to a study of advanced finance and instituting more ways to save, increase, and manage Jim's salary. I took my role of money management seriously and have come to excel in it—and you can, too!

The How-To's of Beauty

My prayer for you is that you won't be like I was—a carefree, uninformed wife who threw up her hands saying, "Oh, I don't know anything about the money! My husband takes care of all of that!" These words might have sounded like respect and submission to some, but they were actually words of ignorance, foolishness, immaturity, and weakness.

My prayer is that you will learn how to increase revenue and make a contribution to your budget whether you're married or single. Here are some steps you can take toward becoming a beautiful money manager, an unfailing prize!

1. Own the assignment—Obviously you will want to follow your husband's desires when it comes to this vital area of money. But you can understand financial matters, know how to handle them, and make your contributions (don't forget those grocery store coupons!) even if your husband does all the paperwork. You can find unlimited ways to contribute if you first own God's assignment to become business minded, to make a contribution in the area of finances.

2. Bone up on money management—Read and collect information on personal finance. Learn what others are saying and doing to manage, earn, and save money. For starters, put into action the "Building Your Own Nest Egg" ideas you read about at the beginning of this chapter.

3. Talk it over with your husband—If you're married, you need to follow your husband's leadership (Genesis 3:16; Ephesians 5:22-24). He's the head of the household and you are his householder, his manager (1 Timothy 5:14; Titus 2:5). So before you attempt a "takeover" or institute any major financial reforms, be sure he approves of the plan.

I put these first three how-to's together and began reading books and articles about household budgeting during Jim's years in seminary—years when we had next to no money! One article I found suggested "Fifteen Ways to Put More Money in the Bank."[3] I implemented the ones I could (like saving sales receipts for tax deductions on April 15), but I took other ideas to Jim for his consideration and input. These more complex proposals involved our joint property. I wasn't about to decide on my own whether we should raise the deductible on our car insurance and drop collision and comprehensive insurance on older cars. I'm sure you get the picture about how and when to get your husband involved!

4. *Get set up for better money management*—Start some kind of record-keeping system. See what a local stationery store or office supply center has available. Look for books on tracking your expenses. Consider investing in a bookkeeping program for your computer or look into on-line banking. Ask your bank about computerized bill paying. Arrange for bill payments to be automatically deducted from your checking account. (I was thrilled yesterday to sign up for this kind of service through our local gas company! That's one less bill in the mailbox, one less check to write, one less stamp to purchase, one less due date to worry about, and at least 15 minutes redeemed!)

Besides gathering knowledge and supplies, you may need to set up a desk area, a specific place for you to sit and manage your finances. Let this be the place where you put everything related to money management, where you perform the actions involved in managing your finances, and where you can file and find important information.

Once you own God's assignment, learn more about money management, agree with your husband on your role (whatever *he* determines it to be!), and get set up, you will be making an important contribution to your household. I guarantee it!

An Invitation to Beauty

Well, I know it isn't at all glamorous and it doesn't seem very lovely, but God considers your contribution in the financial arena of your home quite beautiful!

Dear one, this book is all about virtue, character, godliness, and spiritual beauty. But keep in mind each step of the way that God's kind of beauty is lived out in practical life, in practical places (at home), and in practical ways (money management)!

So glance again through those sacred verses, Proverbs 31:10-31. Ask God's Spirit to open your eyes to the many references to this beautiful woman's thrifty and wise money management. She was truly an unfailing prize to her husband and a tribute to her God. And that's what I want for you!

-5-

A Spring of Goodness
HER MISSION

೧

"She does [her husband] good and not evil
all the days of her life."
Proverbs 31:12

As I sit at my desk and begin a chapter about God's beautiful Proverbs 31 woman who does her husband "good and not evil all the days of her life" (verse 12), I've decided to christen it "A Spring of Goodness." This title is prompted by the two framed photos of my smiling husband Jim that sit on my desk. I snapped the two shots at En-gedi where the Old Testament hero David hid from King Saul and his 3,000 mightiest hand-picked warriors (1 Samuel 23:29–24:2). Jim stood in the exact place for both pictures—but each has its own tale to tell!

In the first picture, Jim is standing in front of a rushing torrent of water falling 100 feet into a teal blue pool. We visited this basin of refreshment on the same day we climbed Masada, the day's second dusty, dirty, dry, and, of course, steep trek! The trail was also very rocky. In fact, this place was a perfect hideout for David exactly because of all its rocks and caves. After trudging up, up, up, and up, over, and around rocks and boulders, we finally reached our destination—these life-giving waterfalls of En-gedi. En-gedi means "fountain of the wild goat" (you have to be one to get there!)

51

or "spring of the kid."[1] And it was definitely a refreshing sight for sore eyes—and a refreshing treat for tired feet!

The small year-round spring that feeds these falls creates a cool, calming, and invigorating oasis in the desert wilderness. Laughing children splashed and played and entertained themselves. Adults waded, relaxed, and soaked their weary feet. A shadow cast by the shear rock wall and the lush green undergrowth and trees served as a cool, welcoming embrace after a day of physical exertion, heat, thirst, and sandstone. How easy to imagine what this refuge meant to David! That one little spring provided everything he needed for safety, for life. David may even have been looking at the rocks around the spring when he described God as his "rock and fortress" (Psalm 31:3), "the rock that is higher than I" (Psalm 61:2).

Now let me tell you about the second photograph. Jim stood in the same spot, but turned his body 180 degrees. The background for this picture is the Dead Sea, a body of water so vast that it claimed the full expanse of my camera range! Forty-nine miles long, ten miles wide, and 1,300 feet deep, the Dead Sea is fed by the Jordan River at the rate of six million gallons of fresh water a day. But the Dead Sea is a salt sea and therefore virtually useless. As the saying goes, "Water, water, everywhere, but not a drop to drink!" Situated in an arid desert land, parched for lack of water, the Dead Sea is good for nothing. There is so much of it, it's so blue and so inviting—yet it poisons those who drink! Truly it is a Dead Sea . . . and a sea of death!

A Heart of Goodness

Now let's return to the picture of the woman who is beautiful in God's eyes, the woman of Proverbs 31:10-31. A faithful mother—who herself is living out God's picture of true beauty—is impressing upon her royal young son what really matters in a wife. She's showing him snapshot after snapshot of God's beautiful woman so he'll recognize her when he sees her.

With this next picture in the album, with the snapshot of verse 12, we peer right into the heart of God's beautiful woman, and we're startled because it is so clean, so pure, so lovely. Hers is a heart of goodness! How refreshing in this day of selfishness—of self-centeredness, self-confidence, self-esteem, self-image, and self-assertion—to come across a selfless spring of goodness. No wonder this woman is beautiful in God's eyes! But how is her heart of goodness demonstrated?

The presence of good—"She does [her husband] good," Proverbs 31:12 tells us. God's beautiful wife is intent on lavishing every possible good upon her husband. She lives to love him, and so she does him good at every opportunity. She operates her life and his home in a way that routinely benefits him with good.[2] Her waking prayer each day is to do her dear husband good—to love him, serve him, honor him, advance him, spoil him, and ease his life. Far from looking for any payoff, notice, or praise, she finds following through on God's assignment to do her husband good reward enough!

And where does all her goodness come from? How can she keep up this kind of giving for a lifetime? First of all, as God's beautiful woman, goodness is part of what God weaves into her character. Doing good is who she is; doing good—no matter what—is what she's all about! Besides, she's a woman who fears the Lord (Proverbs 31:30), and He is the One who calls her to do her husband good. She takes seriously her God-given mission to be a spring of goodness in her marriage. After all, *her heavenly Lord* has ordained goodness as her behavior toward *her earthly lord,* her husband (Proverbs 31:12). And she finds her highest happiness in doing just that—and doing it "heartily, as to the Lord [her heavenly One] and not unto man [her earthly one]" (Colossians 3:23).

The absence of evil—"She does her husband good and *not evil*" (Proverbs 31:12). As a fallen creature (Psalm 14:1; Romans 3:12,23), God's beautiful woman of Proverbs 31 experiences the same temptations toward evil that you and I do, but—by God's grace—she stands strong against them. At every opportunity to give in to selfishness, resentment, anger, disapproval, or disagreement, she perseveres against evil and instead chooses to follow after God's plan to do her husband good—not evil. As one gentleman notes, "Life is difficult enough for a man who makes his way in this world without adding to that burden a wife who does not understand or support him."[3]

The influence of a lifetime—The good which the Proverbs 31 woman does her husband and the evil which she doesn't do are to characterize "all the days of her life" (verse 12). That's the timeframe God has for her mission: She is to overflow with goodness into her husband's life "all the days of her life"! She is to take seriously and literally her marriage vows to do her husband good "till death us do part." Being a spring of goodness for her beloved husband is her lifelong calling. She is to be sweet tempered and constant today . . . tomorrow . . . twenty years from now . . . fifty years from now . . . until death parts the partners. Sickness, poverty, old age, and mistakes are not to dampen her commitment to be a positive influence in her husband's life.

An Example of Goodness

For years I've enjoyed the daily blessing of the devotional series *Streams in the Desert* by Mrs. Charles E. Cowman.[4] For a long time, though, I had no idea what soil her powerful words of comfort grew out of! Only later did I learn her story and, with it, the how and why these volumes of hope and comfort were assembled.

Charles Cowman was founder of the Oriental Missionary Society. As he neared the end of a five-year Gospel crusade in Japan, he commented to his wife, "I have been having such heart pain at night." Despite agonizing physical pain, Charles completed the crusade. Then he returned to the United States for rest and recovery . . . only to suffer a severe heart attack and a paralyzing stroke. His time of chronic illnesses and suffering was truly like nights without stars—six years of them!

To counter their despair, Lettie Cowman determined to use God's promises as an antidote. Collecting countless books and magazines, she searched for words that would encourage both of them, and she read those words day in and day out to her suffering husband. In the darkness of her sorrow, she dug brilliant nuggets of hope out of the rich mine of God's promises to share with her dear Charles. Studying the Scriptures, she found the soul-sustaining power and comfort they both so desperately needed.[5]

Dear one, Lettie Cowman was not only a solid rock for her husband's soul, but she was also a spring of goodness until his dying day. When he was healthy, she was his helpmate in Japan. But in his twilight years she remained loyal to him and to her Lord, spending six years of her life bringing spiritual refreshment to her dear and dying husband. While managing his home, his finances, and his ministry organization during those dark years, she also fed her husband's soul divine truth.

I pray your heart is moved by this beautiful woman's strength. And I trust you are beginning to grasp what a real-life beautiful-in-God's-eyes woman looks like. She's tender, but she's also tough (ever the army)! She's a rock, but she's also a spring. Prompted by God and empowered by a heart full of His goodness, she bears down, follows through, and finishes the task. She's on a mission from God to "do her husband good" (Proverbs 31:12), and she takes that mission seriously, faithfully working to fulfill it.

I don't know what Lettie Cowman looked like from the outside, but you and I do know her heart. I don't know anything about her physical stature, but you and I do know about her strength to endure, to serve, and to remain loyal to her husband to the end. Like all of God's beautiful women, Mrs. Cowman spent "all the days of her life" (Proverbs 31:12) living out God's plan that she be a perpetual spring of goodness to her husband. In Mrs. Cowman's case, her life was indeed a stream in the desert!

The How-To's of Beauty

How can you live out a lifelong ministry of refreshment to your husband?

1. *Beware the enemies of goodness!*—"She does her husband good and not evil all the days of her life" (Proverbs 31:12). Imagine "good" and "evil" in the same verse! These are such sharply contrasting behaviors—the one so desirable and the other so dreadful. Obviously the possibility of a wife doing her husband evil is a reality or God wouldn't mention it. In fact, the Bible itself offers plenty of examples. Scan this list of women who failed to be a spring of goodness for their husbands.

- Eve, created to be a helper for Adam, invited him to join her in her sin (Genesis 2:18 and 3:6).
- Solomon's wives drew his heart away from God (1 Kings 11:4).
- Jezebel stirred up her husband Ahab to commit acts of abominable wickedness (1 Kings 21:25).
- Job's wife counseled him to "curse God and die" (Job 2:9).
- Rebekah willfully deceived her husband Isaac (Genesis 27).
- Michal despised her husband David (2 Samuel 6:16).

What are some heart-issues that could cause such chaos in a marriage? First of all, *a tendency to compare* leads us down a dark path (2 Corinthians 10:12). I know how easy it is to compare my husband, my life, my marriage, my financial condition (the list can go on!) to other people. Comparisons—as well as expectations, dreams, and fantasies (all of which come with disappointment guaranteed!)—can quickly change my heart that should be focused on God's personal plan for *my* life . . . with *my* husband . . . in *my* God-ordained circumstances . . . as I travel on *my* God-appointed mission of goodness.

Why not pause right here and thank God for your husband and for the path He has put you on? While you pray, make the commitment to tend to your tendency to compare! At the same time, decide to do a better job praising your husband and thanking him for contributing to your welfare.

Nurturing *a growing root of bitterness* is another sure way to foster evil rather than good. Allowing bitterness to even begin to take root—bitterness toward our husband or our circumstances—causes trouble and ultimately defiles other people, especially those closest to us, especially our husband and our children (see Hebrews 12:15).

So once again turn to God in prayer and thank Him for every detail of your life. Gratitude that has us looking to God—not our husband or our circumstances—is the weapon with which you and I can do battle against any budding bitterness. Try it. You'll find that you simply cannot be thankful and bitter at the same time!

Finally, watch out for *a sagging spiritual condition.* Problems in a marriage may point to problems in the spiritual life. Staying close to God—by reading His Word, by praying, and by walking in His grace—fills our hearts and makes them the

spring of goodness we desire them to be. The following prayer
focuses on the vital link between living close to God and lavishing goodness on our precious husbands. (Only the gender
has been changed!)

> That I may come near to my husband, draw me nearer
> to Thee than to him.
> That I may know my husband, make me to know Thee
> more than him.
> That I may love my husband with the perfect love of a
> perfectly whole heart, cause me to love Thee more
> than him and most of all.
> That nothing may be between me and my husband, be
> Thou between us, every moment.
> That we may be constantly together, draw us into sepa-
> rate loneliness with Thyself.
> And when we meet breast to breast, O God, let it be
> upon Thine own.[6]

Please make this prayer your own. Allow God to fill your
heart with His great love until it is filled to overflowing as a
spring of goodness right into your husband's life. I invite you
to pray this prayer and pray it often!

2. *Follow God's plan*—Our mission of fulfilling God's pattern for goodness in marriage is empowered by Him when we
plan and practice goodness.

Plan to do good—A wise proverb says, "Do they not go
astray who *devise evil*? But mercy and truth belong to those
who *devise good*" (Proverbs 14:22). Sharing his insights into
this verse, a visiting preacher at my church pointed to Adolf
Hitler, the Nazi leader who masterminded the murder of six
million Jews. He noted that Hitler "devised evil," that he
planned evil, as meticulously as a bride plans her wedding.

What are you planning? You and I can choose to plan for good or plan for evil, but as God's beautiful women we are called to do *good*! So make it your goal to set sail today—and every day—on a course of doing your husband good all day long.

Practice your plan—Don't be content with merely planning to do good. Follow through on your good intentions! Put your plan to work. Hopefully, the following ABCs will help your spring of goodness to gush!

Some ABCs of Goodness

A Always contribute spiritually. Don't discourage your husband about God's plans as Job's wife did (Job 2:9).

B Bless his name. Allow "the law of kindness" (Proverbs 31:26) to rule your words whenever you talk about your husband.

C Control your spending. Be sensitive to the family's financial situation.

D Discipline, raise, and train his children. Proverbs 31 is the faithful teaching of a godly mother to her husband's child.

E Encourage his dreams. Fan the flames of his personal aspirations.

F Follow his leadership. Eve brought sorrow of heart to her man—and to the world—by not following him.

G Give your husband the joy of a happy home. Don't be the contentious, brawling wife of Proverbs 19:13.

H Habitually exhibit a steady, predictable, even-keeled nature. Be sure there's no Dr. Jekyll and Mrs. Hyde in your home!

I Indulge in praising him. A *good* word makes a heavy heart glad (Proverbs 12:25). Let your mouth be a spring of goodness!

J Join him in sexual pleasure. Rejoice his heart and satisfy him "at all times" (Proverbs 5:18-19).

K Keep up your spiritual growth. Seeking the Lord regularly is the best way to contribute goodness to your husband.

L Look not at what others have. Be content—and delighted—with your husband's provision for you.

M Make prayer a part of your ministry to your husband. Nothing creates a deeper spring of goodness in a heart!

N Now try your hand and heart at finishing this alphabet of goodness! Refer to it daily—and, of course, do it!

Just a note here. I know that Proverbs 31:12 refers to the husband mentioned in verse 11, making its application obvious for married women. But Proverbs 31:10-31 is every bit as much a description of a single woman as it is a married woman. Remember that the young man hearing these instructions from his mother was single, and he will be seeking these virtues in an unmarried woman! Clearly, God's goal for all of His women—married or single—is that we be a perpetual spring of goodness!

An Invitation to Beauty

Now, my beautiful friend, can you look full into God's wonderful eyes of love and wisdom and choose to do good (and not evil) to your own dear husband? Even if he doesn't seem so dear to you right now, you are still to be a refreshing spring of goodness to him. After all, your husband is a part of God's sovereign plan to grow you into a more beautiful woman. That growth may mean some stretching, some reaching, and it will definitely mean some heavy-duty dependence on God's beautiful grace. But know that blessings untold await you as you follow God's plan for greater beauty, and that plan includes doing your husband good.

So, regardless of the details of your marriage, realize that your husband is the husband God wants you to devote "all the days of your life" to "doing good" to. As you draw upon your resources in Him, the strength of the Lord (Psalm 62:7) and the mind of the Lord (1 Corinthians 2:16) will sustain you, and He who is always faithful will fill your spring of goodness to overflowing.

-6-

A Fountain of Joy
HER HEART

"She seeks wool and flax,
and willingly works with her hands."
Proverbs 31:13

*J*oin me for a moment or two on a walk Jim and I took through the streets of Old Jerusalem. It was not a pleasant walk (adventurous, yes; educational, yes; pleasant, no!) as our senses were assaulted with various sights, sounds . . . and smells!

Crowds of people were everywhere—shoppers jostling us in their hurry, merchants and hawkers shouting and grabbing at us as we passed by their wares. Animals used for transportation and delivery purposes made their different noises—and left various sights and smells behind! Raw meat with the accompanying layers of flies grew old and rank with the heat of the day. Vegetables and fruit, too, began to droop and reek.

In the midst of this sea of humanity a thousand buses were belching fumes and depositing tourists, dump trucks were contributing their diesel fumes, and the sounds of construction work came from the renovation sites. Add to this scene the midday heat, the relentless sun, and your incredible thirst—and you may have a sense of our experience. And there was no relief in sight!

And then our guide Bill led us through one of the many closed doors that line the streets of the Old City . . . right into paradise! Suddenly—in a single second—we found ourselves standing in the walled courtyard of a home with a flower garden and a small patch of lush, green grass. Blooming vines grew up the walls in the shade of several olive trees and palm trees. Seven pillars supported the second story of a U-shaped, three-sided structure (I was reminded of the home in Proverbs 9:1!), and their graceful arches shaded a walkway. In the very center of this lovely scene was a fountain! Imagine—coolness and shade and water and grass and greenery after the dust and heat of the street! Imagine—silence after the clamor of the crowds, hawkers, and animals! Yes, it was paradise!

But I want to tell you more about that fountain. In the architectural tradition of its day, the entire house, the verandah, the garden, and the walkways were built around that fountain.[1] Singing with joy, that fountain provided the only sound we heard. With its gurgles and gushes, its bubbles and busyness, that lovely fountain said, "Welcome to a place where everything is cared for and every care met!"

When I think of this fountain, dear one, I think of you and me. You see, as God's beautiful women, you and I are to be the fountain of joy at the heart of our home, the center of all that is beautiful and the hub of all that happens there. Proverbs 31 is all about being a fountain of joy—of life, of love, of nourishment—for others. That's why I'm praying that we will each be a fountain of joyful energy, a joyous heart at the center of our home, a faithful and diligent worker who willingly, enthusiastically, and continually makes home happen.

A Willing Worker

The primary ingredient for success in any venture is hard work, and that is especially true when it comes to running a home. In this verse, the wise mother painting the Proverbs 31 portrait addresses the ideal heart attitude God's ideal woman would have toward this hard work: "She *willingly* works with her hands" (Proverbs 31:13)! The woman for her son would be a willing worker, one who tackles her work diligently and cheerfully. She literally "puts her hands *joyfully* to work"[2] and makes her hands "active after the pleasure of her heart."[3]

Exactly what kind of activity is this diligent woman involved in? Weaving is a major part of the work the Proverbs 31 woman has to do (verses 13, 18, 19, 21, 24). The Jewish women of her day were responsible for making the clothing for the family,[4] and wool and flax were the two basic elements needed for weaving. So, with energy and enthusiasm, "she seeks wool and flax" (Proverbs 31:13). After first gathering these unrefined substances, God's beautiful woman then carries out an entire manufacturing process. She starts with raw materials and ends with finished garments—choosing, buying, processing, dying, spinning, weaving the cloth, and finally making the clothing. And Proverbs 31:13 says she does all this with willing hands and a joyful heart!

Throughout Israel's history, much of the people's clothing has been made out of *wool.* The large outer garment common to the region called for this heavy, warm fiber. Those willing to do the work—and God's beautiful woman is!—would dye the wool as they prepared it. Under the keen eye and in the skillful hands of the Proverbs 31 woman, her threads turn brilliant crimson (verse 21), canary yellow, Phoenician purple (verse 22), and dragon's blood red. Then they are ready to be passed through her creative heart and hands, first woven and then made into clothing. Decked out in these colors, her family is quite spectacular against the backdrop of her sun-drenched land.[5]

The Proverbs 31 woman also works with *flax*. She uses the fiber of this slender herb for spinning, but it has to be gathered, separated, twisted, and bleached before it can be woven into fine linen and used to make inner garments, tunics, and sleepwear (verse 24). Processing the flax involves the painstaking steps of drying, peeling, beating, combing, and finally spinning it. In fact, the more flax is beaten, the more it glistens.[6] But no labor was too taxing for our model of a joyful and willing worker!

A Worker of Beauty

Many women do the chores at home because they have to, they're expected to, or they're told to. But the woman who is beautiful in God's eyes throws herself wholeheartedly into her work. Like that fountain in the center of the garden, at the heart of its home, she joyfully sings, hums, and whistles as she works, delighting in her work. She lives out God's exhortation, "Whatever your hand finds to do, do it with your might" (Ecclesiastes 9:10). Far from murmuring at life's demands, she sets a worthy example and finds pleasure in the work of her hands. With zeal, enthusiasm, and gusto, she puts her heart into her work. She goes all out. She doesn't merely do her work; she does it willingly and joyfully!

Our beautiful woman's heart is a fountain of joy. She is filled with love for her God (verse 30), love for her family (verses 28, 29), and love for her home (verse 27). Graced by this love in her heart, she lives a life that overflows with energy, industry, delight, and creativity. Her willing heart transforms her approach to even the mundane chores in her home. This powerful joy of her heart energizes her hands for willing labor.

Some scholars have translated verse 13 to read that the Proverbs 31 woman works with the *pleasure* of her hands, with *willing* hands, with *merry* hands, with *inspired* hands![7] I like all of these thoughts and the attitudes they reflect, and I hope you're getting the picture. Her joyous heart and the busy hands it energizes transform everything she touches into something of beauty.[8]

The How-To's of Beauty

When I think about God's beautiful woman and the abundant energy and obvious joy that distinguishes how she does her work, I want it! I want for myself that same kind of energy and joy when I approach the tasks at hand—and I'm sure you share my desire. Well, I've been experimenting over the years with what I call my "attitude helpers." Besides helping me get more work done, they've helped me do my work with a willing, joyous heart. I hope these ideas help your fountain of joy bubble and flow!

1. *Pray daily*—Pray for those you serve and for yourself. Pray specifically about your attitude toward your work. Because God listens and responds, prayer changes things. Our Lord can turn your heart into a fountain of joy. In fact, prayer can give you the God-given perspective that lifts your duties in the home out of the physical realm and transports them to the spiritual realm (see Colossians 3:23 and number three below).

2. *Recite Scripture*—Make a list of verses right out of God's Word that encourage you to be joyous in your work. My favorite is Psalm 118:24—"This is the day which the Lord has made; [I] will rejoice and be glad in it." When we have verses like that in our heart and recite them as we work, we will find ourselves "rejoic[ing] in the Lord always" (Philippians 4:4)!

3. *Do your work as unto the Lord*—When things really seem unbearable and my perspective becomes skewed,

another verse comes to my rescue. Colossians 3:23 says, "Whatever you do, do it heartily, *as to the Lord and not to men.*" I must remember that the *What*, the *Who*, and the *Why* of my work is God Himself! This reminder adds fresh joy to my empty heart.

4. *Tackle your tasks*—As you face each task, make the conscious choice to tackle it energetically, creatively, and joyfully.

Energetically—Whatever chore you face, take on the challenge and "do it with all your might" (Ecclesiastes 9:10)! That's how Nehemiah and the people approached the task of rebuilding the walls of Jerusalem (Nehemiah 2)—with "a mind to work" (4:6)! They were on a mission! And so are you!

Creatively—Thomas Kinkade, the acclaimed "painter of light," approaches each new painting with a creative heart. He developed this approach during the art-student phase of his life when he worked in a gas station. Hear what he says:

> The work was routine, the hours were inconvenient, the pay was minuscule. My surroundings were grimy, the clientele grumpy. And yet I still managed to have fun at that job. I observed an endless parade of humanity who came through the doors. I made up stories about them in my head and sketched them from memory. I played games with myself to see how quickly I could make change or reset the pumps. And I took pleasure in serving, in knowing I helped people get through their day.[9]

You knew Thomas Kinkade as a creative artist. But he is also a creative worker who clearly has a loving heart!

Joyfully—Just as the heart of God's beautiful woman is a fountain of joy, yours can and should be, too. Sometimes when I read this verse about her happy heart, I feel jealous. I want her joy, her willingness to work, the pleasure she derives from what she views as her labors of love. I think key to her joy is the fact that she looks at her work with anticipation rather than dread. She sees tasks as challenges rather than drudgery. Her positive outlook springs not merely from love for her family, but also from her joyful habit of looking at each demanding task of life and deciding to do it, to do it well, to do it unto the Lord, and to enjoy doing it!

5. *Look for the benefits*—I love these thoughts of Edith Schaeffer, a woman who learned how to see the good in the work of granting her husband's daily request for an afternoon tea tray. Here's how she approached the task and the benefits she found in doing so:

> First, I say silently to the Lord: "Thank You that [this] is a *practical* way to serve *You* tea. . . . Thank You for making it so clear that as we do things . . . in service to others, we are really doing it for You."
>
> Second, I go on to remember something of this sort: "Now Fran [her husband] really needs this . . . refreshment . . . a bit of blood sugar . . . good nourishment, too, for whatever is coming next."
>
> Third, I then walk up the stairs . . . think[ing]: "Who is keeping their waistline? Here I am doing my aerobic up-and-down-the-stairs exercise."[10]

Edith looked for the benefits she received as she served others. Doing so can lighten the burden of your tasks (and mine) just as it did for her.

6. *Pause and rest*—There's nothing wrong with a well-earned rest. God warns against idleness (Proverbs 31:27) and a sluggardly lifestyle (Proverbs 21:25), but He never condemns our physical need for rest. So pause when you need to

and refresh yourself in the Lord (Isaiah 40:31). Schedule a nap each day if it energizes your work.

7. *Watch what you eat!*—One year when I was reading through my Bible, I marked every reference to food, and I discovered that food is an important subject in the Bible. What we eat should be important to us as well. A worthy goal is to eat for energy and health. To see if you're reaching that goal, make a practice of noticing your energy levels. Does the food you eat give you energy or put you to sleep? Do you experience low periods during the day? When—and why? Doing God's job assignments with a willing, cheerful, joyous, energetic heart requires physical energy. Be sure you're giving your body what it needs.

8. *Value each day*—I climbed Masada one step at a time, and that's how you and I will achieve the excellence of God's beautiful woman. The Proverbs 31 woman enjoys the rich blessings of her children's and her husband's praise (verses 28-31), but she earned it by willingly doing her work one day at a time and one task at a time. How we live each day is our "one step at a time" toward her excellence and the kind of praise she received.

So what can you do today? How will you live? How closely will you walk with God? Know that He will use this twenty-four-hour period to make you more the person He wants you to be. In God's economy, nothing is wasted, so He's certainly not going to let this day—whatever tasks it holds—be in vain!

An Invitation to Beauty

What a blessing to know that you and I can bring a gift to our home that no one else can offer—the gift of a heart filled with joy! Your joyful heart can minister to the people at home, the place of home, and the work at home.

Such a heart can even help you find joy in the work you do at home. After all, every task you do out of a joy-filled heart greatly blesses those you love and serve. When you serve with a heart of joy, you refresh and revive tired souls and hurting spirits. Like a fountain of refreshing water in the dusty, dry desert streets, a heart God fills with His love ministers life and health. Besides, whether you realize it or not, dear one, your heart attitude determines how much *you* enjoy your work as well as what the atmosphere of your home will be. When you choose to work with a willing, happy heart, *you* become a beautiful source of joy to all, a fountain of God-given joy!

-7-

An Enterprising Spirit
HER PROVISION

᪲

"She is like the merchant's ship;
she brings her merchandise from afar."[1]
Proverbs 31:14

*O*ne Christmas season Jim and I were invited to a special holiday open house at the home of a precious saint, a member of the Sunday school class of seniors Jim was pastoring. As the guests took turns sharing their childhood memories of Christmas, our hostess told her story as well. She described to us a custom in the country where she grew up: On Christmas Eve the wealthy people of the town would open their front drapes and allow others to press their faces against the windows and look inside their elaborate homes. Many times as a child our friend had stood peering through exquisite panes of beveled glass at the furnishings, decorations, Christmas trees, and food in these residences. On that one rare evening of the year, she could look through those windows and admire the bountiful richness of those who lived inside.

As you and I consider how God's beautiful woman provided for her loved ones, I feel as if He is allowing us to press our faces against the windows of her house. Through the window of His Word, He gives us a glimpse of what her enterprising spirit looks like and how it impacts the way she loves her family. We find every beauty and provision imaginable in her home. God's beautiful woman spares no effort to provide the best she can for her beloved family.

A Spirit of Adventure

Proverbs 31:14 reads, "She is like the merchant's ship." This image may not seem too appealing at first, but consider for a moment how the woman who is beautiful in God's eyes is indeed like a merchant's ship. We can easily imagine, for instance, that she scours the marketplace for goods that will enhance the quality of life under her roof. She spares no cost in terms of money, time, or effort when it comes to contributing to the well-being of those she loves.

"She brings her merchandise from afar," verse 14 continues. The Proverbs 31 woman gladly expends her energy to gather up special goods from around the world for her household—and they truly came from afar. Just look at the process!

The ships—Merchant ships have sailed between Phoenicia and Egypt since 2400 B.C. Stopping in every port throughout the Mediterranean Sea, they traded their cargo for other goods. Second Chronicles 9:21 tells us that these merchant ships completed their route once every three years.

The supplies—The long waits, however, paid off in unusual and exotic goods for those at home. The ships that went to Tarshish (modern-day Spain) brought home gold, silver, ivory, apes, and monkeys (2 Chronicles 9:21). Cedar was shipped out from Lebanon. Dye came from Tyre. Spices, nuts, balm, and grain were exported from Egypt. Greece contributed oil, wine, honey, and exquisite pottery to the international marketplace. All kinds of woolen goods, pieces of art, hand-crafted objects, and exquisite jewelry were transported—sometimes by desert caravan, other times by boats via canals and rivers—to the ports of each continent to be loaded onto the merchant ships.

The superhighways—Merchandise brought into seaports was then carried by caravan back to the inland cities. In fact, ceaseless camel-caravans flowed through the homeland of our beautiful woman. Throughout history Israel has been at the crossroads of every major trade route in the Middle East. When I was there, I traveled the King's Highway and the Great Trunk Road, the two key routes which made the Promised Land a world trade center.

The shops—Finally, after all the caravans and ships, goods from around the world arrived in small shops of all sizes, shapes, and styles. Permanent shops opened onto a square or street, creating a bazaar or arcade in a central location. Portable shops were set up under makeshift awnings near city gates and in the open streets. And whenever a camel caravan arrived from points as far south as Sheba (modern-day Iran) or as far east as Babylon and India, a market appeared instantly wherever the camels knelt. Imagine the buzz of excitement as dry goods, grocery items, tin utensils, leather goods, sweetmeats, and other valued rarities arrived by camel in the village streets!

A Spirit of Mission

Now, my patient friend, let's look more closely at how our beautiful woman from Proverbs 31—*like* these merchant ships—is on a mission to bring her merchandise from afar. *Her family* is the primary reason she searches far and wide. She has mouths to feed and a house to furnish and decorate—and, as she sees it, her loved ones deserve nothing but the best. So, motivated by her heart of love, she goes the extra miles (literally!) to provide the best for those at home.

But the Proverbs 31 woman is also motivated by her *creativity*. She's an artist! Let me give you an example. Since her home has no refrigeration, she shops daily for the ingredients she needs for each day's meals. This responsibility could easily become a drudgery, but shopping at the exotic foreign market booths feeds her imagination—and her family—and allows her to express her creativity in day-in-day-out life. In those stalls she discovers color, beauty, and variety, the unique, and the exquisite. This adventure stimulates creativity in her recipes and meals, her weaving and homemaking. Mundane, routine, daily provision became a creative adventure for her!

A Spirit of Satisfaction

This book is about beauty as seen through the eyes of God, and here we are, talking about . . . shopping! But realize the enterprising spirit of this woman who is beautiful in God's eyes sets her apart from others. Like the merchant ships of her day, she sets sail and glides on and on . . . searching . . . looking for . . . seeking out . . . and obtaining what she wants to provide for her family. Motivated by love for those she cares for, she sets forth on her mission with vigor and anticipation, willing to explore beyond the familiarity and convenience of her neighborhood market. She "sails away" to the faraway corners of the city and returns laden with exactly what her family needs. As she puts forth the effort, this special homemaker enjoys a sense of satisfaction as she provides what's best for her family:

- Health resides under her roof because she sets nutritious foods before her family.

- Savings result as she searches, bargains, and barters to provide the necessary and the beautiful for her clan.
- Culture enters her doors as she brings home not only goods from far-off, exotic places but also the tales heard and the information gathered while making her purchases.
- Variety spices up life in her home as foods and furnishings from afar greet and treat those within.
- Quality goods are enjoyed by all because of her keen eye and uncompromising standards.
- Beauty satisfies, invigorates, and ministers to the souls who abide there.

The How-To's of Beauty

By now you and I can sense that the enterprising spirit which God holds up to us in this chapter doesn't come without effort. A sailing vessel doesn't just naturally or automatically cut rapidly through the waters with its sails billowing! Such beauty comes at a price for the Proverbs 31 woman (and for us, too). Having caught a breeze stirred up by her busyness and bobbing in the wake of her energy and accomplishments, look at how—in God's grace—you can nurture such an enterprising spirit and then set sail on your own.

1. A heart of love—Without love we are nothing (1 Corinthians 13:2), and, I might add, without love we will want to do nothing! So . . .

Pray—Ask God to reveal and heal any area in your heart that keeps you from loving your roles as a wife, mother, and home manager.

Make home your first priority—Even if you aren't within its four walls as much as you'd like to be, cherish your home and those who reside there. Your family—not your job or profession, your hobby or your volunteer work—is to be first in your heart!

Spend time with other women—Listen to other women who speak with heartfelt love about their husband, their children, and their home (Titus 2:3-5). You'll find their enthusiasm contagious.

2. *A vision of loveliness*—God's beautiful woman appreciates beauty and its ministry to those it touches. As a creative individual, nurture your own vision of loveliness and offer your family your personal expressions of beauty.

Surround yourself with beauty—When confined to his bed in his later years, the great Impressionist artist Henri Matisse, ordered exotic plants and brilliantly colored parrots brought into his bedroom. These additions stimulated the art he produced from his sickbed during those final years. Inspired by Matisse, I painted my office walls red, hung them with my favorite pictures and paintings, and decorated with objects (a calendar featuring great art of the world, a crystal bud vase with a single fresh cut rose, a rock found on the West Texas prairie by my aunt and painted to portray a kitty curled up in its basket for a catnap) that push me to be more creative. Cocooned in loveliness, I seek to produce what is lovely. My office itself invites me to write.

Make your vision of loveliness a reality—Spend time with people who are creating beauty. Study magazines. Visit gift shops and attend home shows. Pay attention to any loveliness you encounter along the way and learn from what you see. Finally, let the furnishings and decor of your home be an expression of beauty.

I remember so well coming back to my own home after staying in the house of a woman who had a vision for loveliness, and I had been changed by my visit. When I stood at the entrance to her living room and took in the exquisite beauty that welcomed me into the haven she had created for her family, I thought, "Why, she's an artist!" My initial impression wasn't of money spent; I didn't think, "Look at all the stuff she's bought!" Instead, I was struck by the arrangement of things—by little touches like placing Grandmother's lovely hand-crocheted doily on the arm of a chair, displaying a shell found on the beach, and having a low-hung lamp spotlight a tiny table and its miniature fern. She had also removed some curtains so that the containers of exotic, blooming kaffir lilies lining her porch seemed like part of the room. And she had sparkling clean windows. This woman with a vision for loveliness had simply taken what she had, tweaked it a bit, and made it remarkable!

3. God's assignment to love—Love your family in the practicalities of daily life.

Start with the basics—Every individual needs the basics of food, clothing, and shelter. As one author asks, "Are you too tired to cook meals and keep the house in order? Do you want to eat out all the time?"[2] Or are you energetically providing the basics your family needs?

Become a wise shopper—Focus on saving money. Look for bargains. Avoid impulse buying by carefully considering every purchase (Proverbs 31:16). Know what you need and what you don't need. Learn what is quality and what isn't—and also how to say no! Remember one of the keys to money management: all money not spent is money saved! Sometimes I say no by deciding not to shop at all. Other times I say no by shopping by catalog, foregoing the time and temptations of wandering through stores and malls. Still other times I say no by seeing how many things I can take out of my shopping basket before I go through the check-out stand, and then I mentally add up my savings.

Search for the unusual—Wait a little longer and search a little farther until you find something basic that's also a bit unique. The Proverbs 31 woman shops in the city's *bazaar,* but she is looking for the *bizarre!* Ever the artist, she has an eye for the unusual. She delights in picking up the odd item, something imported, something sure to bring oohs and aahs from family and friends—and that something rewards her enterprising spirit!

Consider bartering—List your skills and then seek to sharpen them. They will be your currency as you barter for what you need. So figure out what you need and what you can give in exchange for it. Bartering like that has worked for me. My book *Loving God with All Your Mind*[3] was first transcribed from my teaching tapes by a seminary wife from New Zealand in exchange for a used car my husband made available to her husband for three years. They needed a car—and had no money. I needed help—and had no money (or time). So we bartered!

Become "the resident artist"—Consider yourself on assignment to bring beauty into your home. Once a week my friend Karen—the resident artist in her home—sails away at 4:00 A.M. to the flower mart in downtown Los Angeles to bring fresh flowers into her home and onto the patio and porch. (She also uses the flowers to make bouquets for those who need a little beauty to cheer them up.) By the time I call her at 7:30 A.M., Karen is already busy adding touches of beauty here and there throughout her home—and she's doing this for just pennies! Karen challenges herself to do something new and creative in her flower arranging week by week. Like Karen, figure out exactly how you—the resident artist in your home—can create beauty there. Also ask yourself, "What area of creativity could I work on improving and developing?"

An Invitation to Beauty

Now, my beautiful enterprising friend, it's time to look deep into God's eyes of love and acknowledge the desires of His heart for your life. Through His Word, our wise Father calls you to be an enterprising homemaker and wife who adds touches of beauty to her home. This call requires some effort, but it's a call to great blessing!

Is your heart in tune with God's great heart of love? Do you cherish those at home whom He has given you to provide for? Are you giving your utmost as you work to provide for your family? Proverbs 31:14—albeit an image of a merchant ship—actually addresses a matter of the heart, a matter of love. You see, only love—God's gracious love—can motivate you to lay aside selfishness and exert the physical energy needed to set sail on behalf of others. And only the love of God, filling you to overflowing, can supply you with the necessary emotional endurance to forego personal ease and sustain the relentless activity of a lifetime of enterprise for the good of others.

Won't you ask God to give you greater resolve and renewed energy so that you can sail off toward the endearing—and enduring—quality of an enterprising spirit? Truly, such a spirit is beautiful in God's eyes!

-8-

A Pattern for the Household
HER DISCIPLINE

"She rises also while it is yet night,
and gives food to her household
and work to her maids."[1]
Proverbs 31:15

I couldn't sleep—and a full-blown case of jet lag was the reason! Jim and I had arrived in Jerusalem the day before after 15 hours of flight time and a stopover in London. We had already been awake for several hours in our hotel room inside the Old City of Jerusalem, waiting for daylight and an excuse to throw on some clothes and begin our 21-day study course in the Holy Land. We'd been too tired the day before to appreciate much of what we had taken in through blurred eyes, but now we were ready—if the sun would just come up!

Finally there was enough light to merit a walk up to the roof of our hotel. Standing shoulder to shoulder in the dawning light, we heard church bells from distant corners of the Old City heralding a new day. As the sky brightened in the east, we could see the centuries-old walls fortifying the Old City of Jerusalem, the flags flying atop David's Citadel, and a panorama of the Temple Mount where Christ had

83

walked—and will walk again in the future. It was a breath-taking sight: we were looking at places that haven't changed in hundreds of years! We were in Jerusalem!

Then I saw her. On a rooftop nearby a woman was hard at work. Her laundry was already hung on a line. Her front door was open, allowing the morning air to cool the stone house before the day's heat set in. Her porch was already swept and scrubbed, and now she was at work on her rooftop. Cutting some fresh flowers that grew there in pots, she then carried them into her home along with several ripe lemons picked from her rooftop citrus trees.

This opportunity to watch a real-life Jewish woman brought Proverbs 31:15 alive—"She rises also while it is yet night, and gives food to her household and work to her maids." The spectacular view I had been enjoying made me glad I had gotten up early (although jet lag gets most of the credit!), but now I was freshly challenged by this hard-working woman to keep on trying to live out the kind of disciplined life that is beautiful in God's eyes. "Thank You, God," I whispered, "for the Bible made alive! Thank You for this glimpse—here in Your land—of a woman who gets up early and lovingly tends to the ways of her house."

This chapter is about how you and I can lovingly tend to the ways of our house. The beautiful mother who is teaching her son the ABCs of godly womanhood (Proverbs 31:10-31) knows full-well the benefits a well-disciplined woman can bring to her household, and she points her son (and us!) to three disciplines for a woman's success in the home.

Discipline #1: An Early Start

According to Proverbs 31:15, the woman who will bless her home "rises also while it is yet night." Back when Proverbs 31 was written, a woman got up early for a number of reasons.

Tending the fire at home—First, she tended the lamp. This small lamp (more accurately, a saucer filled with oil with a wick of flax floating in it) was kept burning all night so that the household fire could be lighted from it in the morning. God's beautiful homemaker got up several times during the night to replenish the oil so that her lamp didn't go out (Proverbs 31:18). These night risings were also ideal opportunities to get a headstart on some of the food preparation for the next day. She could grind a little corn, set a few things out, and lay the fire.

Tending the fire of her heart—Proverbs 31:30 says that God's beautiful woman fears the Lord, and an early start gave her time to tend to her daily prayers and the keeping of God's Law. She knew the Law said to love the Lord with all your heart, soul, and might (Deuteronomy 6:5). Our Proverbs 31 woman must tend not only the fire at home, but also the fire of her own heart's love for the Lord.

Tending the fires of their hearts—This godly woman also knows that the Law of Moses instructed her to teach and train her children in the knowledge of God and His laws (Deuteronomy 6:7). God's beautiful mother first fills her own heart with God's truths. Then, just like the careful mother teaching Proverbs 31 to her son, she teaches those truths to her children and talks of them all day long in the classroom called "home."

An early start is essential when these crucial tasks are on your list!

Discipline #2: Food for the Family
The woman who is a blessing in her home "gives food to her household" (Proverbs 31:15). Her family's daily bread was a major reason for her early rising. They depended on her

to provide them the food they needed. Even today three out of four people in the Middle East live entirely on bread and other foods made from grains.[2] Bread was—and is—truly the staff of life and a mainstay with every meal. And there can be no bread until the grain is ground (the first duty of each day). Then the dough is mixed, and finally the small pita-like flat breads are baked on hot rocks and ashes.[3]

But there is an exciting image behind this verse! The Hebrew word used here for "food" actually means "prey" and refers to the prey of a lion. God's beautiful woman is likened to a lion hunting for the prey it needs to survive. She is pictured as a lioness prowling at night ("she also rises while it is yet *night*") to obtain food for her household.[4] Besides being an army (Proverbs 31:10), a warrior (verse 10), a worker (verse 13), and a powerful ship (verse 14), she is now a lioness (verse 15)! The images of these verses continue to point to her tremendous strength and courage. The prowess of this woman is so great that she provides for the needs (food) of the others (household) under her charge.[5]

And that "household" includes anyone fortunate enough to be under her roof on a given day! "Household" is a collective term used for a unit of people, a group, everyone in the entire house.[6] Her list of lucky VIPs includes her husband (her most important VIP), her children (these junior VIPs are next in line), any extended family (in those days many family members lived in the same house), her servants, and her guests.

Discipline #3: A Plan for the Day

"She gives . . . work to her maids" (Proverbs 31:15). "Work" or "portion" refers to something due to another, a prescribed portion or allowance.[7] It's assumed that God's beautiful woman gives a portion of food to her maids as members of her household, but she also gives them work. She issues them a "decree" or work "ordinance" which outlines their daily work assignments.[8] She has her own work to plan and organize, but her maidservants also need their assignments—their "portion"—for the day (verse 15). Eager not to lose a minute of the day's work time, she has to be ready for them—early!

A Pattern for Success

God's beautiful woman lived out a pattern for success that worked in her day and time, but you and I can have success today, centuries later, by following her pattern for her household: She got up early (a simple but not necessarily easy thing to do!). Just count her many blessings!

Time alone—A chief complaint I hear among women is that they have no time alone. It seems the kids are always there (with their needs—and noise) and the phone is always ringing (with still more needs—and more noise). The TV is usually blaring (more noise!), and Mom just never seems to find any peace and quiet. Early rising gives you that cherished quiet time. In the still of the pre-dawn morning, you can have some precious time alone.

Time with God—When you get up a little early, you can use the time to seek the Lord and spend a few moments in prayer, asking His blessing upon your day and your household. A Mother's Day article I read featured an interview with Anne Graham Lotz, daughter of Ruth Graham, who wrote of her mother: "No matter what time I arose in the morning, I would see the light from [Mother's] room. When I arrived downstairs she'd be at her desk reading one of 14 different Bible translations. This was one way Mother taught me that it is through the Word and prayer that I can know God. She knows God well."[9] (And she rises early to do it!)

Time to plan—In your time alone, you also have time to think, and that's how effective planning gets done. A few quiet minutes alone before the rush of the day begins means time for the planning that is essential for a well-ordered home. Hear one top time-management expert's praises of early rising: "I do almost all my planning early in the morning. I . . . average . . . three and a half hours a week at it. I wake up around 5 A.M., before anyone else in the house, and I put this quiet time into my most important activity—planning."[10]

Time to get the jump on the day—There's no doubt that getting up early starts a chain reaction of benefits. Rising early is your first step toward redeeming time! Look at what that time can mean for you: Time with God—for guidance and strength. Time alone—for planning. Time to exercise—sometimes it's the only time! Time to get a jump-start on the day—for wise use of the hours to come. Time for breakfast—for fuel. Time for family devotions—for focus as a family. When you make early rising a discipline for each day, you take an important step toward setting an orderly tone and establishing a predictable pattern for your household.

A Personal Story

Thanks to my husband, Jim, I regularly experience the benefits of early rising (most days, anyway)—and let me tell you why.

As a new seminary student, Jim returned home from class each day praising a man named Mr. McDougal. Jim would say over and over, "You have to meet Mr. McDougal! He's a professor, he has a wife and a family, he's a student himself in a doctoral program at UCLA, he runs every day, *and* he pastors a church."

One day Jim finally asked Mr. Don McDougal how he accomplished all that he did. "He gets up every day at 4 A.M.!" Jim exclaimed when he told me the story later. While I was busy thinking, "That's great for *him*," Jim announced, "We're going to start getting up at 4 A.M.!"

Facing such an early hour was difficult (and still is!), but the benefits were immediate. For one thing, that much-sought-after time with God became a reality. Suddenly I had time to linger in God's Word and I had time for unhurried prayer. Furthermore, for the first time ever, I was able to plan my approach to the hectic day ahead, a day filled with young children and household chores.

But there was even more to be gained by my early rising. I was able to start an exercise program—which I still follow each morning. I could also unload the dishwasher, make all my phone calls to eastern time zones before 8 o'clock, do our bookkeeping, write letters, type, file, study the Bible, and create Bible study materials—all before 7:30 in the morning. Even today I have a file labeled "Early A.M." and keep in it an ongoing list of the tasks I can do early each day.

So, if you want some time without any interruptions, some time of quiet peace and solitude, try rising early in the morning. You may have to get to bed a little earlier. But after all, what are you missing? Perhaps a little TV? You do need time for family, but you'll be surprised how much time you can buy back from non-essentials when you are motivated to get up early.

Well, Jim graduated from seminary many years ago, but I still try to get up early. Like the woman on her rooftop in Jerusalem, I open up all the doors and windows in the summer to cool the house. I, too, get my laundry started and water our flowers. Although I don't grind grain, I do grind our coffee beans and get the coffee pot going for Jim. When Katherine and Courtney were at home, I checked on them and then shut their doors so my early-morning noises wouldn't disturb them for the few extra minutes they had before their alarm clocks went off . . . and they, too, rose early!

What are some of the "noises" I make around our house in the morning? Well, the coffee bean grinder! (After all, first things first!) The opening of windows and doors. The running of sprinklers. The emptying of the dishwasher. The setting of the breakfast table. The making of lunches. The taking out of trash. The hum of the treadmill if it's a bad-weather/no-walk day.

And the noises cease and all gets quiet—very quiet! Then, before the onslaught of another day's busyness, I sit down and worship the Lord and behold His beauty (Psalm 27:4). You see, I know what's coming! My day will be fast-paced and full. If I'm not "full" myself, I'll fail to handle the day's demands in the beautiful way God has in mind. Going to Him for strength is not an option—it's a must! I know I can't be the warrior I need to be, I know I can't even make it through the day, if I don't have the strength and courage only He can give me. I can do all things beautifully—including handle one more frenzied day—only through His strength (Philippians 4:13). His peace is not an option either. I know there's only one way to conquer anxiety—and that's by receiving from God His peace which passes all understanding (Philippians 4:6-7). Do you see why my early morning hours are priceless?

The How-To's of Beauty

I'm sure you've heard a lot about getting your beauty rest, but it's much more important to be getting God's kind of beauty by rising early. Of course you need to rest, but early rising brings the beauty of order and discipline to life. So instead of living a life marked by the helter-skelter of things lost, forgotten, or misplaced, characterized by running behind and never getting around to it, and punctuated by "oops!," "eek!," and "oh, no!"—cultivate the discipline of getting up early. How?

1. *Determine a time*—You probably won't start your day at 4:00 A.M. (we did because Jim had to leave the house at 5:30). But figure out what time you want to have completed your planning, your preparations for the day, and your ideal morning routine, and then work backwards. That's the time you need to get up. When you do, I bet you'll love having a schedule that works—and so will your family!

2. *Get to bed*—You can only burn your candle at both ends for a while before you burn out! So try moving your bedtime up an hour. At least be *in* your bed an hour earlier!

3. *Say a prayer!*—Pray as you turn out your light. Center your day's-end thoughts on the Lord and all you desire to accomplish for Him and His kingdom with your upcoming fresh new day. Your lights-out communication with God sets your mind on the next day's work and transfers something physical—getting up a little earlier—into the spiritual realm.

4. *Get up!*—And thinking about the amount of life you're buying back when you get up early is certainly motivation to do just that! A time-management authority says this:

> [If you] can do nicely with six hours of sleep instead of the eight you now may be getting, saving those two hours a day, Monday through Friday, would give you an extra forty hours—one additional work week—every month! . . . Just one hour less sleep per night would mean: six extra work weeks per year, which adds up, over a working lifetime, to more than five years. Think what you could accomplish in an extra five years!—"Up and at 'em!"[11]

An Invitation to Beauty

My dear and beloved reading friend, I hope you're catching a vision of the important role you play in your home. Oh, you may have a job, a career, even a prestigious title outside the home, but even so *you* are the key to a well-run home, the key to the order and efficiency of your entire household! In the words of this chapter's title, *you* set the pattern for your household. So when you take (and make) the time to plan, to organize, to micro-manage for the smooth functioning of your home, you give your family—and yourself—a gift no one else can give them. You give your husband the gifts of peace of mind and a sense of order and well-being as his heart trusts and rests in your management. And you give your children a pattern for how to run their own lives. As they watch you plan and manage and then taste the sweet results, they learn how to live their lives for the Lord.

God's beautiful Proverbs 31 woman models for you (and me) the discipline of early rising. Time spent praying and planning in the early hushed part of the day gives you a master plan that works for your home and sets a pattern of order for your life.

So, as the time-management expert advised, "Up and at 'em!"

-9-

A Field of Dreams
HER VISION

∾

"She considers a field and buys it;
From her profits she plants a vineyard."
Proverbs 31:16

*A*rtists like my friend Margaret tell me that the
most difficult part of the human anatomy to
draw is the face. Mastering the skills to accurately represent facial features is the final frontier for any
artist. As you and I enter this chapter about the Proverbs 31
woman, we begin to see her face take shape as a few revealing
characteristics are sketched for us. So far we've watched her
hands work with delight (verse 13), marveled at the heart
her husband trusts (verse 11), and been impressed by her
swift feet as they take her afar for her family's provisions
(verse 14).

But now the mind of God's beautiful woman is opening
up to us as He, the Original Artist, reveals its impressive abilities. In the preceding chapter we watched her use her keen
mind to plan and organize. Now, in verse 16, we see that she
uses her mind as a visionary *and* a businesswoman.

You may have heard about the findings of "right brain-left
brain" research. Supposedly one side of the brain controls our
creative functions and the other all that is *practical*. Well,
God's beautiful woman has fully and gloriously developed

93

both sides of her brain! In the creative realm, she's a visionary—a person given to dreaming and imagining.[1] She wants what's best for her family and dreams of making that "best" happen. But she doesn't stop there. She puts the practical part of her mind to work to make her dreams happen. You see, she's a businesswoman as well as a visionary.

Triple Action

Although this chapter is about dreams and visions (and active imaginations!), we can learn much from the three concrete actions which God's beautiful woman takes in Proverbs 31:16 as she works to make those dreams come true. The same three steps can help you and me make our own dreams become reality.

Step #1: Consideration—Imagine the following scene. Our beautiful woman of Proverbs 31 rises early one morning, feeds her family, sees her husband off to work, sets her servants into action, and, like that merchant ship, sails out the door on her rounds of daily shopping. While she's conducting business in the town market, she hears about a local field that's just come up for sale. Heart racing, she discreetly asks a few questions and gathers some preliminary information about the property.

Why the racing heart? Because she has a dream—a vision born out of love—that will better her dear family. She's always been on the lookout for a chance to make that dream happen, and this field definitely looks like a golden opportunity to increase her husband's wealth and status and thereby improve her family situation. But how does she respond to news that the property is for sale? Does she impulsively rush to the landowner and buy the field? Does she reach into her tunic, whip out her clay credit card, and blurt "Charge it"? No.

"She *considers* a field," the Bible tells us (Proverbs 31:16). Donning her businesswoman hat, she carefully looks at the field to determine whether or not it would be a wise investment. In her heart, she wants a field, but choosing instead to let her mind take control (like a good soldier), she sets out to learn all she can about the piece of land.

- The value of the property—Collecting information about said property, she *considers* its worth. Not relying only on hearsay or even on expert opinions, she examines the land for herself.

- The state of the finances—Evaluating the family finances, she *considers* whether there is adequate money to purchase and improve the property without endangering the family's welfare.

- The inventory of time—She *considers* her time commitments to her family to determine whether she has the time which the ownership of the field would require.

- The review of priorities—Her family is her primary area of ministry and responsibility, so she wisely *considers* whether working on the field will threaten those priorities.

The Proverbs 31 woman realizes that she has much to learn, ponder, and pray about before she makes any kind of real estate investment.

Finally, after due consideration and consultation with the Lord, I believe she brings the matter to her husband. Armed with a businesswoman's facts and statistics, she shares her vision. Laying out her report, she points to the many reasons why this property is desirable and exactly how it will benefit her husband and the family.

Now why would this very capable woman go to her husband? I can think of several reasons—all of which are entwined in her great strength of character. *As a woman of virtue* she doesn't act independently from her husband, her God-ordained head (Genesis 3:16). *As a woman of strength* she doesn't act impulsively (Proverbs 19:2). *As a woman of wisdom* she doesn't act without advice (Proverbs 12:15). And, *as a wife*, she doesn't want what her husband doesn't want (Proverbs 19:14). God's beautiful woman lives her life to please God, and a part of pleasing God includes pleasing her husband (Genesis 2:18). She is a team player, wanting what her husband wants and helping him move in the direction he's chosen for his family. Together they are a solid unit, so they move forward . . . together! They build their life . . . together! They make their dreams come true, hers of increased financial strength for her family (verse 16) and his of service in his community (verse 23) . . . together!

Blessed with his approval (how could he not approve, what with her track record, her business head, her work ethic), she takes the next step toward owning her field of dreams.

Step #2: Acquisition—"She considers a field and *buys* it," Proverbs 31:16 reports. As one scholar remarks, "There is no way we can interpret this to say less than what is obvious. This woman apparently does buy and sell land. . . ."[2] In verse 16, the term "buys" is from the business world, denoting buying and selling, the give-and-take of business dealings.[3] So we see that the Proverbs 31 woman takes possession of her field of dreams.[4]

Before I traveled to Israel, I had always imagined her field as being something of a ranch or a farm. But after seeing the fields of the Holy Land, I now know that her field was basically a lot, a piece of land measuring about 50 feet by 80 feet.

Each owner first cleared the area of its many large rocks and used them to build a stacked-stone wall around the lot. Then the owner tilled and planted the land. The work was difficult, tedious, and time-consuming.

But where, we wonder, does God's beautiful woman get the money to buy a field? How does she finance her field of dreams? The cash comes from her shrewd money management. Her thrift pays off in daily life as well as in this business deal. All her efforts—her management, her work, her industry, her bartering, her weaving, her sales, her doing without, her saying "no"—furnish the capital that make her dreams come true. As someone has said, "Hard work is the yeast that raises the dough!"

Step #3: Renovation—"She considers a field and buys it," Proverbs 31:16 says; "From her profits she *plants* a vineyard." Despite what this verse seems to suggest, two different pieces of property and two separate business transactions are referred to here. "Field" and "vineyard" are different words for distinctly different kinds of property. Our beautiful woman does not purchase a field and then plant a vineyard there, but rather she purchases both a field and a vineyard.[5] With her hard-earned, well-managed, faithfully saved money, she not only buys a field but also selects and plants a vineyard with the best plantings her funds could buy.

Why a vineyard? Her choice of crops was wise. In her dry homeland where water is so scarce, grapes and wine were staples. Everyone needs fluids to drink, so by owning her personal vineyard God's beautiful woman takes care of her precious family. What is leftover she sells to others, earning more money for her next dream. Everyone benefits! "With the fruit of her hands" (KJV) she plants "fruit" so that her family will be well supplied with the essentials as well as the conveniences of life.

The How-To's of Beauty

When you and I, in quest of our dreams, seek and follow God's wisdom and add our own hard work to the pursuit, everyone benefits. Here's a beauty plan for making your dreams come true.

1. *Desire God's beauty*—Ask the Lord to build in your heart a treasure-house of beautiful virtues. Ask Him to supply you with:

- Patience—so that you will wait before you act when opportunities arise
- Prudence—so that you will carefully think things over while you're waiting
- Prayerfulness—so that you will seek the Lord's wisdom while you are waiting and thinking
- Petition—so that you will willingly consult your husband—or parents or pastor or boss—after you've waited and thought and prayed
- Purpose—so that God will guide your heart in the right direction, in His direction
- Perseverance—so that you will do whatever it takes to make your dreams come true

2. *Devote yourself to God's goals*—And that means family comes first! Your goal is to build your house (Proverbs 14:1), build an honorable name for your family (Proverbs 22:1), and build up the next generation (Proverbs 31:28). Never mind what you're going to get in return. Don't worry about what your building efforts will cost you personally (and I'm not talking about financial cost!). Forget about whether or not others will be grateful for your selfless service or whether they will even notice it. As God's beautiful woman, you don't do what you do to *get* anything: You do what you do because of

who you are, because of the person God is making you into—a virtuous woman, a woman who is beautiful in His eyes! Selfless service is the greatest beauty of all. It's the beauty of our Lord!

3. *Your husband is paramount*—Remember how "the heart of her husband safely trusts" the Proverbs 31 woman (verse 11)? In verse 16, we've seen another way that trust is built. That way involves your willing submission and subordination of your personal desires to those of your husband. Note again that this is done willingly. (God's beautiful woman does everything willingly—verse 13!) As you strengthen godly virtues and put them to work in your everyday life, and as you consult with your husband on the issues at home, you, too, will build his trust in you. Your husband will be smiling inwardly as you present your cases. He'll be trying to keep a straight face, thinking, "Here she goes again! She's truly amazing! Where does she get her ideas? And where does she get her energy?! I sure am fortunate to have her as my wife!" He'll be like the husband of Proverbs 31:28-29 who praises his wife as "the best of all."[6]

4. *Creativity abounds!*—As you continue to set self aside and serve others, you'll be surprised by the multitude of opportunities God gives you to creatively show your love. Your mind and heart will burst forth with "hidden art" (as Mrs. Edith Schaeffer calls our creative efforts in the commonplace activities of life).[7] Consider the source of the ideas I heard about recently at a time management seminar for busy women. Do you know where the speaker learned the magical methods she was passing on to us? At home—organizing a home, a husband, and five children! I've also been in classes like "Cooking Meals in Under 20 Minutes." It's the

same success story: Some super-busy, pressed-for-time woman discovered creative shortcuts as she served her family.

My special friend Kris, with three little ones and her husband still in school, purchases her children's clothes at "The 99¢ Store" and pulls out her hot-glue gun, a few doo-dads (spare buttons, a dried flower, a leftover piece of rick-rack) and creates stunning clothes for her children—for next to no money! When she caught a vision for what she could be doing, her field of dreams became an ongoing booth in a craft fair. Now she sells her creative efforts to other moms for their children—and helps pay for her husband's education at the same time. A business was born in the kitchen as Kris stood at the ironing board. Her dream came—and then became a reality—because all the necessary ingredients were present: focus on the family, loving provision, dutiful service, and a spark of creativity!

5. *Dare to dream!*—If you could improve your family's financial status, what would you love to do? Combining your love for family, the personal desires of your heart, and your own creative bents, what direction would you go? Like the Proverbs 31 woman, who is both creative (verses 13,18,21-22,24) and driven to provide for her husband, children, and home, you can use your creativity for practical purposes.

So don't forget to dream! God's beautiful woman's supervision of her home, her oversight of the budget, her labor for her family, her doing without, her thrift, her saying "no," and her time spent getting the best bargains—all of these efforts pay off in money saved and lead to her dream becoming reality. Clearly, one of her financial goals is earning and saving money she could use not for herself, not for trifles, but for making her dreams for her *family* come true! Because of her dreams, her *family* is served. *They* benefit.

Their life is improved. It's crucial that you, too, be ever-conscious of money. You just may want to follow your dreams someday, so be sure you'll have the finances to help your dream take shape.

6. *Do the work!*—How do dreams become reality? The progression for God's beautiful woman went like this:

Her virtue (verse 10) led to
    her willing heart (verse 13), which led to
      her industry (verse 13), which led to
        her savings (verse 11), which led to
          her investments (verse 16), which led to
            her prosperity (verse 25).

Behind every success story is plain ol' hard work—powered by love for family, a vision of their well-being, a dream about how to make that happen, and God's gracious blessing!

An Invitation to Beauty

Now for you, my friend with hidden talents galore! I could be writing these same beautiful truths about *you*! I want you to dream right now, to consider your field of dreams. Turn off the TV. Turn off the radio, the music, whatever it is that keeps you from thinking creatively, from dreaming and wondering and planning.

Now describe your dream—or ten of your dreams! Then start through this process for making your dreams come true: *First, consider your dreams.* Pray. Count the cost. Pray. Gather information. Pray. And talk to your husband. *Next, do the work.* Money comes from hard work, so do what you need to do in the way of saving, earning, and managing. Once you have the finances, you can begin the work of acquiring your "field," your materials, your start-up supplies. *And move forward*. Be careful not to neglect your home or family. After all, you're taking on the dream to benefit them. You're not on this earth to primarily build a business: You're building your house (Proverbs 14:1), an honorable name for your family (Proverbs 22:1), and the next generation (Proverbs 31:25, 28)! So, I repeat, behind every success story is plain ol' hard work—powered by love for family, a vision of their well-being, a dream about how to make that happen, and God's gracious blessing!

-10-

An Eager Attitude
HER WORK

⌒

"She girds herself with strength,
and strengthens her arms."
Proverbs 31:17

I smile every time I think about the results of a survey I took several years ago. During a teaching series entitled "The Wise Home-maker," I asked a hundred women just like you and me, "What keeps you from getting your housework done?" Their answers fell in this order:

#1 Reason: Poor use of time

#2 Reason: Lack of motivation

#3 Reason: Failure to plan

#4 Reason: Procrastination

I'm smiling and nodding now because I can certainly relate! The items on the list make perfect sense to me!

Here's how the progression usually goes for me: My poor use of time is always linked to a lack of motivation, indicating to me that I'm unsure about what I'm trying to accomplish! You see, when I don't know *why* I'm trying to accomplish something, when I have no goals or only unclear ones, I remain totally unmotivated and use my time poorly.

And planning? Well, doesn't a lack of goals mean that there's nothing to plan for—or at least an uncertainty about what to plan for?

And then there's procrastination. I certainly put off what I'm not sure I'm trying to do. As I said, it all makes perfect sense to me.

So, if you're like me, dear friend, you and I can both thank God that He has shown us His beautiful Proverbs 31 woman who uses her time—indeed, every second of it—and uses it well! She knows her goal: She's on assignment from God to build a home (Proverbs 14:1) and is therefore highly motivated. She wisely plans her days so that each one of them moves her toward her goals and dreams. She works— and she works *hard*—never procrastinating, always using her time well, focusing her plans and her energy on making her dreams come true. I hope you join with me in a heartfelt "Thank You, Lord, for Your beautiful woman!" Where would we be without her model and inspiration?

As we've looked at Proverbs 31 verse by verse, you and I have marveled at the two sides of God's beautiful woman: She is both mentally tough and physically strong, as her attitudes and her work reveal. We see these two sides again in verse 17, looking first at her mental strength, her attitude. You see, without mental toughness, we'll never get around to doing the actual physical work!

Preparation for Work

How does God's beautiful woman—whom we've seen described metaphorically as an army, a warrior, a ship, a lioness, and a farmer—get her work done? What is the key to her success in all that she tackles?

First, "she *girds herself* with strength," Proverbs 31:17 tells us. These words, carefully chosen by the female teacher, suggest the *attitude toward work* her young son should look for in a wife. Let me explain the imagery.

Three thousand years ago when this poem was written, women (and men) wore flowing garments. To perform physical labor, they had to first gather up their dress and secure it with a girdle-like belt. Only then would they have the unlimited movement they needed for heavy labor. This girding of the gown was necessary preparation for serious work[1] as well as prolonged effort.[2]

The girding action was also a psychological trigger for her attitude. Much like putting on an apron, work clothes, exercise clothes, painting clothes, or gardening clothes, much like rolling up your sleeves, the action of gathering one's dress was key to preparing to act. This preparatory action and the appropriate clothes encouraged a "let's go" attitude toward the task at hand.

Second, "she girds herself *with strength*" (Proverbs 31:17). The Hebrew emphasis on the Proverbs 31 woman's physical strength and endurance suggests her unwavering commitment to work and her ability to work hard. A part of her strength comes from her *choice* to engage in hard work, and the girdle is a symbol of the mental and physical strength she wears as she enters the arena of her labor. Her girding herself with strength reveals that she is motivated to do her work and prepared for the activity. This phrase could also be translated, "She dressed herself in strength!"[3] The Bible speaks of "strength unto strength" (Psalm 84:7), and that's what God's beautiful woman enjoys: As she disciplines herself to work, that discipline results in greater strength and endurance![4]

Finally, we see that she "strengthens her *arms*" (Proverbs 31:17). This reference to her physical strength tells us that she is ready to work. She has prepared herself for the effort physically as well as mentally. Like a lioness, she is physically able and strong.[5] As one translation exclaims, "How briskly she girds herself to the task, how tireless are her arms!"[6]

A Personal Formula for Work

If I were paraphrasing Proverbs 31:17 today, I would say, "When it comes to work, the woman who is beautiful in God's eyes is ready, willing, and able!" As I've thought about this quality in God's beautiful woman, I've decided that her mental attitude is the key to the volume of work she accomplishes, and that attitude reveals the following four qualities of the heart.

Commitment—Work is a matter of the heart, and where there is no heart commitment, little (if any) work gets done. I know in my early homemaking days I had to make a commitment to step into the homemaking arena. I loved reading, brooding, and watching TV. But one evening I heard a Christian woman I admire say, "I don't do anything sedentary!" I thought about that statement for days (and I still think about it—and her—every day!), and I finally made a pledge to be more active, to keep moving, to always be doing something. After all, as another proverb teaches, "In all labor there is profit" (14:23)!

Willingness—Our willingness to do the job plays a large role in how easily we accomplish our work and how much we get done. We can have a heart commitment to do the work, build the home, serve the family, and carry out God's plans, but we must also be willing to actually do it! As a woman of God, a virtuous woman, we've enlisted in the army, so to speak; we've signed on; we've volunteered. So now we have to be mentally ready and willing to do or give whatever is necessary to answer the call to duty!

Motivation—For me, motivation is key to the work I do because motivation is the "why" of anything I do. I'm constantly thinking and praying about what I want for my life, my marriage, my family, and my home *and* what I want to contribute to my church, to God's people, and to others. I want what the Proverbs 31 woman reaped in her life: to have God as the driving force behind all I do; to enhance Jim's life; to give the church, the world, and the next generation two godly daughters; to give the gift of order and beauty in the home to my family; to be a generous giver of whatever my church needs me to give; and to touch the lives of other women with the love of Christ. Beloved, this is what I want (and I think it's what God wants), and I want these things badly enough that I'm motivated to do the work—from sunup to sundown—to make it happen (Lord willing!). These goals provide motivation for a lifetime, and give me strength of mind as I tackle the work involved.

Discipline—Ouch! For me, this is the one that hurts. Up to this point, everything has been dreams, desires, goals, and talk! But, as the second half of Proverbs 14:23 so rightly states, "Idle chatter leads only to poverty!" Discipline is necessary for turning talk into action and reaching goals. Here's how it happens for me. I can want a clean house, but discipline is what gets me out of bed when the alarm goes off. Discipline is what gets me up off the couch or out of the easy chair. Discipline is what makes me walk over to the pantry and pull out the vacuum cleaner and cleaning products. Discipline is what keeps me moving when I want to take a break. Discipline is what pushes me to finish fully instead of leaving some things undone or done halfway. Discipline is what makes me put everything away when I'm done!

And this discipline is all a matter of the mind! We fight the battle to get any kind of work done in the mind. That's where we make our choices; that's where we decide how to spend our time and energy. That, my fellow pursuer of beauty, is why mental toughness is basic to work. When we're mentally tough, we'll win the battle over laziness, procrastination, disorganization, and other enemies of productivity.

The How-To's of Beauty

Let me pass on some methods that help me "work up" a better attitude and even an eagerness about my work.

1. Embrace God's will for your life—If you're uncertain about what God's will for your life is, you're seeing it expressed right here in Proverbs 31. So study these verses of the Bible carefully. Put the message in your words and then own it, love it, tackle it, be committed to it, and dedicate your life to it!

2. Stay in God's Word—Allow the Spirit of God to energize your heart, mind—and strength—through the power of God's Word. After all, fundamental to who she is, God's beautiful woman loved and feared the Lord (verse 30). Her goals were derived from His Word, her strength was empowered by His Word, and the grace to persist was given through His Word and His Spirit!

3. Develop a vision—Having a vision of the big picture, of your goals, of the ministry possibilities of what God is calling you to do, will mean an eagerness about what you're doing. Think for a moment about how your daily environment is a direct result of your vision for your home and family, your vision for the beauty and order of a well-run home and for peace under your roof. Broaden your horizons and also nurture a vision for the future of your family members and the contribution they can make to society. Allow a prayer like this one to fuel your vision: "Lord, make us masters of ourselves that we may be the servants of others."[7]

4. *Tap into the why*—I may be repeating myself, but it's vital to know *why* you are doing what you do. The *why* will motivate the work. Some unknown teacher has accurately set forth this truth: "The secret of discipline is motivation. When a man [or woman] is sufficiently motivated, discipline will take care of itself." You can know what needs to be done and possess all the necessary skills to get it done, but until there is motivation—an understanding and passion for the *why*—the job probably won't get done!

5. *Pray for an eager attitude*—When you turn off your light at night, pray about the work that awaits the next day. Ask God to help you greet the day with an eager attitude (see Psalm 118:24). Then, when the alarm wakens you, thank God for another day in which to serve Him and love your family.

6. *Create a schedule*—A schedule will help you plan your work. You'll know what's coming and where you're going, and you'll be able to anticipate the pace and envision your next task.

7. *Develop a routine*—The more work you're able to fit into a daily routine, the better. Those things you do everyday (spending time with the Lord, getting dressed, exercising, making coffee, watering the lawn, unloading the dishwasher, making the bed, bringing in the newspaper, tidying up, fixing breakfast, lunch, and dinner, running errands, etc.) take less

time when they're part of a routine. Your goal is to be able to say, "This is when I *always* walk . . . tidy up . . . pay the bills. This is the day I *always* clean the house . . . get the groceries . . . wash the clothes . . . pull the weeds." Then you'll be able to glide more effortlessly from one task to the next. Also, because you're used to your routine, you'll have fewer decisions to make, less thinking to do, and less indecision to battle. You'll perform many tasks by rote, leaving your mind free to pray, dream, and plan. Knowing what's coming can also generate an eager and energetic expectation about the next tasks.

8. *Read books on time management*—Proverbs 31 is a portrait of the excellent woman, the excellent wife, the excellent mother, the excellent homemaker, *and* the excellent time manager! She's the best of all, and that's God's challenge to you and me. So study organizational systems and make them work for you. Learn the best, fastest, most effective and efficient methods for doing your work. Reading about time management will stimulate your eager attitude *and* offer tips on improving your skills so that you, too, can excel in your work!

9. *Tackle the worst first*—There's no reason to live your days under a cloud of dread because of some challenging or unpleasant task you need to tackle. Simply do that task first! Having the monumental thing out of the way makes the day go more smoothly and easily. Having cleared the major hurdle of the day early on, you'll have fresh energy as you dive into your more pleasant work.

10. *Play music*—One afternoon at about 3:00 I called my friend, another Karen. I had to wait a moment while she turned her music down—one of Bach's lively Brandenburg concerti. She explained, "I always play loud music in the

afternoons when I start to sag. It keeps me going!" That's good advice. Try it.

11. *See how quickly you can work*—Try to beat the clock. Better your times. Make doing your chores a game. The reward is having more time for your own creative pastimes and your field of dreams. With your housework done, you can concentrate on a cottage industry just as God's beautiful woman did with her weaving. Besides, just thinking about topping off your day with such pleasure will fuel an eager attitude for your work.

12. *Consider yourself*—Consider the message in this poem and pray that you will not be your own roadblock.

> All that stands between your goal
> And the deeds you hope to do
> And the dreams which stir your soul—
> Is you![8]

An Invitation to Beauty

Thank you for staying with me! I so desperately want you to make it to the peak of this woman's glory! I'm excited about this woman who is so beautiful in God's eyes, and I'm trying so hard to capture some of her beauty that I sometimes think smoke is coming right off these pages!

As I was just now re-reading this chapter's section on motivation (please read it again!), my heart was freshly moved for you. I know I was listing all the things I want for *my* life, but, beloved friend, I passionately want them for *you*! Why? Because these selfless acts of generous love are what *God* wants from us—and we are supremely blessed when we walk in His paths (Psalm 16:11).

I also want you to experience the unutterable joy and ful-fillment that come from acting on the desires of your heart, desires which God has placed there (Psalm 37:4); I want you to experience the exhilaration and continuing motivation that come with such noble efforts. So please pause, pray, pour out your heart to God—with tears if they flow—and, relying on His grace, persist in the divine work God has given you to do for Him!

-11-

ℋ Taste of Success
HER CONFIDENCE

cᘔ

"She perceives that her merchandise is good,
and her lamp does not go out by night."
Proverbs 31:18

ℋs we begin another chapter about true beauty, I want to tell you in advance that this verse may be my personal favorite. I'll tell you why in a minute, but first a few statements.

First of all, I know that each and every verse of this exquisite Proverbs 31 portrait of the beautiful-in-God's-eyes woman is powerful, potentially life-changing, and crucial because it comes from God Himself. I also know from the study of Proverbs 31:10-31 that my husband, children, and home are to be paramount as I live according to His ways. As a married woman, my greatest fulfillment and highest reward come in the arena of the home. Living according to God's priorities brings me real blessing and joy.

But verse 18—this little gem tucked in the middle of this outpouring of instruction—offers me motivation for a lifetime. You see, verse 18 is the spark that ignites the flame of a full-fledged business for the Proverbs 31 woman, for me, and perhaps for you, too. As we've seen, God's beautiful woman does all things well, and she enjoys the success that results from attaining her standards of excellence. We've also seen her

113

willingness to work hard and to save pennies by bartering and bargaining. Through thrift, hard work, and saying "no," she builds a savings account that supplies her with the capital for some real estate ventures. Having taken care of her family and seeing that her home is well cared for, she now starts up her own little business.

Excellence in All Things

How did her business begin? How did it come to be? The wise, royal mother who is teaching this alphabet of wisdom shows us and also offers us a formula for success—in a word, *excellence!* When you and I pursue excellence in all things (Proverbs 31:29), we can experience the kind of success enjoyed by God's beautiful woman.

Excellent taste—Proverbs 31:18 opens with, "She perceives that her merchandise is good." The word *perceive* is the same Hebrew word that is translated *taste* in Psalm 34:8— "taste and see that the Lord is good." So we see that God's beautiful woman tastes and perceives that her merchandise is good. By trial she finds out that her work is good. By taking risks, trying new ideas and methods, and refining her efforts, she learns that what she's producing is good. She can be confident about her work, and she is.

Excellent goods—But what exactly is the merchandise she perceives as good? First, this woman has purchased a field and planted it with crops, and she has planted another field with vines (verse 16). The yield from her land—corn, grapes, wine—is greater than what her family needs, so she sells the extra produce.

This excellent woman also sells her weaving. Remember all her effort processing the raw wool and flax (verse 13), spinning her yarn (verse 19), and weaving it into exquisite works for her family, home, and self (verses 21-22)? Perceiving that her woven clothing is good (she must have gotten a lot of compliments!), she confidently creates and sells her handiwork to others (verse 24).

Excellent results—The merchandise that the Proverbs 31 woman sells is "good" (verse 18). Put differently, her merchandise is *profitable*—and it is profitable because it is *good!* All she does is done first for her family and nothing but the best will do for them. She would never offer her loved ones something shoddy or quickly thrown together. Her standards of excellence mean the work she does is top quality. So, when a little of this "best" is leftover, she sells it. Because her merchandise is good, it has a ready market and brings a good price.

Excellent pursuit—Next, verse 18 reports that "her lamp does not go out by night." God's beautiful homemaker confidently follows through on her financial enterprise even at the cost of late-night efforts. She likes what she "tastes," and that spurs her on to continue her work even into the night. Her creative efforts and the financial gain that results motivate her to even greater industry and diligence. Because trading conditions are good, she burns the midnight oil to make the most of them while they last.[1] Her intellectual perception ("she perceives") turns into physical exertion ("her lamp does not go out by night") as she pushes forward to both benefit her family and express herself creatively in her work.

Before we move on, let me add a quick note about the lamp mentioned here. When dusk arrived, a lamp needed to be lit if any activity were to continue. As I've mentioned, these lamps were actually flat saucers with pinched edges, and they held olive oil and a flax wick. The lighting of the lamp signified several things about a home.

- First of all, a lighted lamp meant that work was going on so light was needed. Much work was certainly going on in the home of God's beautiful woman!

- Hospitality was another reason the lamp was used. Its light signaled to needy travelers that comfort and refreshment were available.

- A light—shining because precious oil was being burned—also meant prosperity (Proverbs 21:20).

- Finally, a lighted lamp meant wisdom: Someone inside had the practical wisdom to keep a lamp burning so that the kitchen fire could be lighted in the morning. And remember who got up periodically during the night to make sure the lamp didn't go out or burn out (verse 18)!

All said, God's beautiful woman is a busy woman, not only giving her maidens tasks, but working herself late into the night as well as early in the morning (verse 15). She works outdoors in her field and vineyard during daylight hours (verse 16) and inside her home day and night (verse 18) as she tends to her profit-making projects.

Well, my dear friend, we shouldn't be surprised that her business is successful. After all, our beautiful woman doesn't avoid hard work—and, in her skilled hands and with God's blessing, it's good and profitable work (verse 18)! She's doing something she enjoys (she works willingly with her heart and hands) at the same time that she helps gain financial security for her family (she does her husband good, and he has no need of gain). She's also free to be creative in her clothing designs, and her management of these efforts makes a profit for her family. The joy of creating and the satisfaction of selling motivate her to continue. On and on the blessings and benefits of busyness and business continue. A cottage industry has been born!

A Stimulus to Excellence

I call the little business of God's beautiful woman her "Proverbs 31 Project." And now I want you to pray about what is it that you do—or might do—to contribute to the finances at home. I hope this roll call of some of the many women I know who work late into the night will stimulate and inspire you. Let their Proverbs 31 Projects spark your imagination and encourage you to keep your lamp burning at night!

- My daughter Courtney oversees the taxes and prepares all the returns for her household, and her Paul gladly gives her any tax refunds as pay. This was the beginning of her own small business—which she does at home—compiling tax returns for others as well.

- A registered nurse I know picks up medical charts from her local hospital every evening, checks them at home, and delivers them the next day with the appropriate paperwork done. She also picks up a paycheck! She simply modified her profession and moved it home when her first baby arrived.

- A seminary wife bakes all her own bread—and takes orders from people like me for their daily bread! She also sends baked goods to school with her husband to sell in the student lounge at break time. Voilà! Money for educational expenses!

- My husband's former secretary took her typing skills home when her first baby came along. She types student papers—and transcribes tapes for me—right from her home!

- Then there's my "pool person" friend! To save money, this true Proverbs 31 woman asked her husband if she could clean and maintain their pool and collect the same monthly fee he was paying a pool man. So she began keeping her pool clean—and pocketing the money for her family's needs. When her neighbor saw her sparkling pool, he asked if she would clean his, too. Today Kathy does every pool on her block, and she uses the money for her family's needs.

• And then there is my Lisa, a sharp woman with a husband, two young toddlers, and a home. But she also has a master's degree in English, a heart filled with compassion, and an incredible ability to write. Lisa is my editor—and a capable editor for many others. She's a master manager of her time and energy and—just like God's beautiful woman (verses 15 and 18)—rises early and stays up late to turn her passion into a profession—and some profit!

In light of these ideas, why don't you take some time to evaluate your dreams, abilities, and interests? Pray about an area you can develop so that you can help improve your family's financial situation and add your name to my list. (If you already hold down a job outside the home, challenge yourself to be more creative once you're home. Don't just give at the office!)

Even as you consider a Proverbs 31 Project, let me remind you that you make a significant financial contribution simply by taking care of the home. We've talked about the money you save by systematic bill paying, wise shopping, careful menu planning, and healthy food preparation. Add to that tasks like yard work, housecleaning, and perhaps cleaning your own pool that you do yourself rather than paying someone else to do. The wise saying is certainly true: "Money saved is money earned."

It's OK if your lifestyle doesn't allow for a formal Proverbs 31 Project. I know that every woman is different, and every woman's situation is different (eight children? no children?). But if God has gifted you with special creative abilities, a mind for business, some marketable professional skills, the blessing of spare time, an empty nest, or some initial capital, by all means think about and pray about how He would have you put these gifts to work for your family.

The How-To's of Beauty

Now some tips on determining your personal Proverbs 31 Project.

1. *Listen to others*—Are you getting compliments for something you do? We usually take our gifts for granted. We tend to think, "Oh, everyone can do this! It's so easy!" and we fail to notice that no one else is doing it—or doing it with the same excellence, flair, or boldness. Sometimes we may even think, "Oh, that's not so great! Others do a better job!" instead of thanking God for the abilities He's given us and trying to use those abilities in a broader way.

2. *Move forward*—Did you goof? Did the recipe fail, the paints run? Were you unable to find the exact words for your writing (I can relate!) or the right notes for your music composition? Did you over-fertilize your prize roses? Move forward from these experiences with the attitude of inventor Thomas Edison who failed thousands of times before he invented the light bulb: "Don't call it a mistake. Call it an education!"[2]

3. *Develop your skills*—To be successful in your Proverbs 31 Project, you need to continue to develop your skills and techniques. My daughter Courtney enrolled in a culinary school to further develop her wonderful cooking skills. She has an ability and the desire to do more in the kitchen, and she has "tasted" enough success to dare to dream of future

enterprises involving food preparation. Whatever it takes to develop your skills, commit yourself to it. You'll not only develop skills but confidence as well.

4. *Redeem your time*—Buy back time from less important activities and use it for your Proverbs 31 Project, for personal creative efforts, for your "merchandising." As I focused my mind and energy on my writing and speaking, I noticed that a few once-regular activities completely disappeared. I no longer spend hours watching television, shopping, attending luncheons, going on outings, or talking on the telephone. One of the few activities I make extended time for now is my "work," and I willingly extend it far into the night! (It's 10:30 P.M. right now!)

5. *Take risks*—Be creative. Try new things. Express yourself. Adopt my friend Julie's attitude toward her flower arranging—"Be bold!" in whatever enterprise you are exploring.

6. *Do your best*—"Whatever your hand finds to do, do it with your might." That's the wisdom of Ecclesiastes 9:10. God's beautiful woman certainly works with all her might and all her heart. All she does, she does with excellence. As a result, her merchandise is good!

7. *Do your projects unto the Lord*—In both the Old Testament and the New, in Proverbs 16:3 and Colossians 3:23 respectively, we are told to commit our work to the Lord and to do our work as unto the Lord. With Him as the reason for your work, with Him as your Boss, with His glory as your goal, you'll experience the blessing of His strength and His guidance. With Him as your stay, you'll also find staying power for staying up!

8. *Manage for profit*—As we see in this profile of God's beautiful woman, profit can be gained in several ways. We can strengthen our family's financial situation by money saved, by money earned, and by money invested.

9. *Know what you're doing is important*—In Psalm 34:8, David calls us to "taste and see that the Lord is good." The meaning of see is "convinced"—and usually the hardest person to convince about the value of your efforts is you! Remember that this chapter is about the confidence of God's beautiful woman—her confidence in her God, her God-given talents and abilities, and her use of those gifts for the good of her family and other people.

10. *Family first*—Jesus teaches that if the tree is good, the fruit will be, too (Matthew 7:15-20). For God's beautiful woman, her family comes first. All that she does, she does for them. Because her family's good is the desire of her heart and the focus of her actions, the fruit of her efforts is good. She isn't motivated by greed, but only by her concern for her dear family. That motivation prompts her to do her best, and God uses her to bless her family and others (Proverbs 31:20,24) in a variety of ways, including financially.

So take a second to check your motives. Are your efforts fueled by the right motives? As my wise pastor exhorts, "You take care of the depth and let God take care of the breadth." In the case of becoming beautiful in God's eyes, you take care of your family and let God take care of how He chooses to bless and expand any business efforts.

An Invitation to Beauty

I hope and pray that, by reading this chapter about God's beautiful woman, you are encouraged to:

- Pour your greatest energy and most fervent efforts into your family and home.

- Pray for discernment about the area you excel in, what area you may be able to expand into a Proverbs 31 Project.

- Pursue your skills and sharpen your expertise.

- Plan for a few late nights of creative effort.

- Prepare to taste success!

-12-

A Little Night Work
HER DILIGENCE

"She stretches out her hands to the distaff,
and her hand holds the spindle."
Proverbs 31:19

It happens every day. The sun that lights the world and energizes our life and our work starts to sink, signaling to our weary minds and bodies that another day is winding down. You and I both know the order of events from this moment on: Soon there will be supper to serve, the dishes and the kitchen to clean up, baths to give, teeth to brush, stories to read, kids to tuck in, and then it will finally be time to call it a day and go to bed.

It's been a long day and a full day—full of challenges, creativity, service, and work. And . . . ooooh . . . it's going to feel so good to be in a horizontal position, to rest our weary mind and body, to draw up the covers and close our eyes—until we rise up before the next new day dawns! These are the kinds of thoughts and feelings that enter our mind via a tired body as God closes His curtain of darkness on the activities of another busy day.

But wait a minute! As we read on in Proverbs 31, we discover an added dimension to God's beautiful woman, another trait that causes us to completely reevaluate how we approach our evenings! Just when you and I thought we were done for the day, God's beautiful teacher presents Lesson #12 (we're halfway through!) on what it means to be beautiful in God's eyes. Her young son listens as she again points to the diligence of the Proverbs 31 woman who does a little night work before going to bed.

Behind the Scenes

It's true that work, work, and more work lie behind every success. You and I are considering the wonderful success story of the Proverbs 31 woman. Clearly, she's a woman of diligence—ever persevering, continually industrious, and constantly busy. Delighting in her family and her work, she rises early to take care of her household and continues to work at the other end of her day, too. She puts her evenings to good use.

In the preceding chapter, we saw that God's beautiful woman foregoes a little beauty rest for a little night work: "She perceives that her merchandise is good, and her lamp does not go out by night" (Proverbs 31:18). But what, we wonder, does she do in the evening? Proverbs 31:19 may provide an obvious answer: "She stretches out her hands to the distaff, and her hand holds the spindle." When evening arrives, God's beautiful woman shifts her activities from outside in her fields to inside her home where she works by lamplight (verse 18). Yes, she's put in a long day, but she keeps on working in the evening. In her day it was perfectly natural and permissible to retire when night fell, but our heroine stays up to work . . . just a little longer.

And, according to Proverbs 31:19, she's working with a distaff and a spindle. Mentioned nowhere else in the Old Testament, these ancient objects were used in spinning wool.[1] In skilled and experienced hands, the distaff and the spindle converted processed wool and flax into yarn and thread. These two implements were definitely the tools of the cloth-making trade for the Proverbs 31 woman.

Earlier in verse 13 we saw that she uses her energy to bring in, dress, clean, and untangle her wool and flax. Now at night, as her body slows down, she sits and spins, perfecting the wool and the flax for her weaving. She knows that the monotonous work of spinning must be completed before she can be more creative and begin her weaving.

This kind of behind-the-scenes preparation is necessary before any great work can be accomplished. For instance, before there can be a painting, the canvases must be stretched and mounted. Before a dress can be sewn, the pattern must be cut out. Before an opera can be sung, the scales must be practiced. Before a book can be written, the research must be done. Before a wall can be painted, the baseboards must be masked. Before a meal can be cooked, the ingredients must be cleaned, chopped, and measured. Such behind-the-scenes work may be mundane, routine, unglamorous, dull, unchallenging, and even a "no-brainer," but such preparation is fundamental to beauty and usefulness.

So God's beautiful woman willingly, cheerfully, heartily, and gladly (verse 13) spends her evenings doing the tedious, unexciting—but very necessary—work from which her great works of art are born.

The How-To's of Beauty

When I first began working at night rather than plopping down in front of the TV with a bowl of Cheetos and a Coke, I struggled! Making the commitment to use my evenings to help my family and ministry and developing self-discipline in a new area, I gradually learned to use my evenings in useful and creative ways. (It's 9:15 P.M. as I write this!) Now I value my evenings that were, for so long, a hidden treasure.

In fact, finding this gift of time for a little night work opened up a whole new life for me. Christian Development Ministries was birthed by Jim and me one evening ten years ago. A wiser use of my evenings has given me the time to sit beside Jim at the helm of our ministry organization and to develop and use my spiritual gifts to enrich the lives of Christian women. I shudder to think what I would be doing (or *not* doing!) if I had continued to throw away God's gift of evenings!

As one time-management expert advises about some often-wasted hours, make your evenings and weekends count![2] Hopefully some of these first steps that revolutionized my life—and my evenings—will encourage you to do just that.

1. *Evaluate your evenings*—I recently heard the highest-paid sports agent in the world talk about a skill he practices every day. Speaking on the importance of time, he stated that he plans his day (every single one of them—even his weekends) in 20-minute increments. Do you know how you spend every 20 minutes of your evenings? Answering this question can be quite an eye-opening exercise!

2. *Plan your evenings*—One Sunday morning at church I walked right past a friend of mine. Thankfully she grabbed my arm as I went by so I could share in a wonderful thing that had happened to her—she had lost 40 pounds! (That's why I walked past her—I didn't even recognize her!) When I asked her how she had done it, she told me that she had decided to exercise every night after she got home from work. Her goal for the new year had been to incorporate that one activity into her life, specifically her evenings. In other words, she planned her evenings—and she's definitely enjoying the payoff!

I try to plan my evenings in advance because, by the time they roll around, I'm too tired to put forth the mental energy it takes to even think about doing something useful! So I created what I call my "P.M. File" (the bookend to my "Early A.M. File"). In my "P.M. File" I keep a running list of activities I can do at night.

For instance, I assemble my Bible study workbooks a hundred at a time. I autograph my books for Bible study groups. About once a week I answer my correspondence. (Sometimes I've dictated so late into the night [I've seen 2:00 A.M. before!] that the words are barely intelligible.) Paying bills, bringing the checkbook up to date, and reconciling our bank statement are good nighttime activities for me. Night is when I go through junk mail and catalogs, keeping a large trash can nearby! Our clothes get folded at night, and any ironing that needs to be done gets done after the sun goes down. As a teacher and writer, I need lots of illustrations, so in the evening I sift through books of quotations, biographical notes, and art books. At night I major on the minors, keeping my reading content on the light side. I save the heavy-duty commentaries and research books for the daylight hours (and energy)! And I don't know about you, but I have lots of piles around the house, so on some nights I sort through a pile or two.

Create your own "P.M. File" and plan your evenings to include a little night work. Your file might include clipping coupons, looking through your recipe box, and making menus. Following in the steps of God's beautiful woman, you could mend, knit, crochet, or do embroidery and cross-stitching. Work on making your Christmas gifts at night—and then wrap them after the sun goes down. Read your favorite magazines, the newspaper, or a professional journal at night. Use the evening to pursue your own special interests. If you like art, classical music, cooking, gardening, or history, why not rent an educational video to watch instead of evening TV? Or listen to an audiotape and take notes.

Maybe you want to watch TV with your family—or at least be in the same room with them. I meet many women whose husbands want them right there beside them on the couch during the evening programs. Well, author Anne Ortlund lists 22 things you can do then. Here's a sampling: Look over your calendar and plan ahead, give yourself a pedicure, write a letter to an old friend, do your nails, bring your recipe file up to date, put all those old photos into albums, polish the silver, and write your pastor an encouraging note.[3]

The point is, my beautiful sister, to save your daylight hours—your prime energy time—for the work that demands the most from you physically and mentally. When dusk begins to darken the day and your energy starts to fade, instead of zoning out, kicking back, and plopping down, follow the example of our beautiful and diligent woman: Simply change activities. After all, Proverbs 10:4 tells us, "She who deals with a slack hand [and is negligent] becomes poor, but the hand of the diligent makes one rich." In other words, the lazy person reaps nothing, but those who are diligent succeed. So plan for diligence!

3. *Prepare for your evenings*—If you set up a "P.M. File," you'll have some specific options for your evenings and know exactly how to plan for them. So before the sun goes down and you get too tired, set out the supplies you need for your little bit of night work. If I'm going to assemble Bible study workbooks, I set up my assembly line right on the coffee table. If I'm working on bookkeeping, I set up the card table in the family room so I can be with my family while I work. I have a friend who created a letter-writing caddie to hold stationery, postcards, notecards, stamps, envelopes, pens, and her address book. You could set something like that by your husband's easy chair and write away. My friend Judy has her art easel standing in her cozy family room. My treadmill and

exercycle are permanent fixtures in our family room—a constant reminder to me to keep trying!

I've even discovered some tricks for getting more done in an evening. One of those tricks is exercising or going for a walk to get my energy level up for the evening's activities. Another trick is telling myself, "Now, Liz, just do one more thing." Whenever I finish one effort, I remind myself that I can do just one more thing. Before I know it, I've been doing just one more thing all evening long! Or I tell myself, "Just five more minutes and I'll quit!" (I once read that "the difference between an amateur and professional is about five minutes more."[6]) And once again, I'm surprised and thrilled when all those "five minutes more" add up to three or four hours of additional work getting done.

4. Use your evenings!—It's great to evaluate, plan, and prepare, but ultimately you must use your evenings. And that calls for effort! God's beautiful woman "stretched out her hands to the spindle" (Proverbs 31:19). What do your hands reach for at night? A snack? Another romance novel? A favorite video? Your pillow? The remote control? This chapter is about diligence; it's an invitation to you to make your evenings productive.

If you hold down a job outside the home, you may find it especially challenging to use your evenings once you're home. Here's how one woman does it, described in a chapter she wrote entitled "Working Women, Read This First."

> The evening? Checking clothing needs and making breakfast preparations the night before. . . . As soon as I greet everyone, I gather up the laundry for the day and start the washer. Then I cook. Dinner is our family time, and I try to keep it pleasant and unhurried. After dinner, I transfer laundry to the dryer and clean up the kitchen.

(Each evening, as I cooked dinner, I mixed up a batch of dough for our traditional Christmas cookies and breads. I refrigerated them all, and then on one night I had a baking orgy.) The cleaning of refrigerator, range, and cupboards, I've moved to evening. Sometimes, if I've had a rough day, I take a 30-minute nap. Right now, with [my] writing schedule so tight, I spend more time at the typewriter. Whatever I'm doing, I keep an ear open for the dryer's stopping so that I can snatch out the clothes. . . . I schedule the last 30 minutes before bedtime for self-improvement. This includes exercises, skin, teeth, and nail care.[5]

This beautiful woman has so many dreams and so much to do that she simply doesn't have time for talking endlessly on the phone, sprawling out to watch TV, or kicking back after a hard day. No, she knows that her home is to be the site of her best work and her true fulfillment. That's one reason why her family time, home-making chores, creative baking, and writing projects motivated her throughout the evening. Once you get yourself going on a little night work, you'll find yourself motivated to continue, too!

5. *Use your mind in the evenings*—Even if you're doing dull, routine work, your mind can be active. With a little prompting, creative sparks can fly while your hands are busy. As God's beautiful woman spins her raw materials, she probably imagines what she could make with the yarn and linen, maybe even pausing to sketch her ideas. Designing in her head while her body rests and her hands sail, she creates her unique garments, deciding which ornaments would complement the fabric, what kind of design to embroider across the yoke, etc., etc. Whatever your "no-brainer" task is, assign your brain a creative task, choose a fun or serious subject to think about, or train yourself to dream!

An Invitation to Beauty

Speaking of dreaming, I want to challenge you to dream! First, name something you love to do, something personal, a passion you carry in your heart. Do you realize you just might be able to turn that "something personal" into "something professional" by doing a little night work? I know many women who have two professions—one by day and one by night.

For instance, my mother was a Shakespearean scholar and teacher by day and a seamstress by night. As I grew up, she made all of my clothes, continuing to send me a package of newly sewn clothes every week I was away at college. Mom used her nights—often until two o'clock in the morning!— to sew all the curtains, throw pillows, dust ruffles, and pillow shams in our home. Her hands worked magic as she made all our bathrobes, even whimsically whipping up doll clothes for my "babies" and a Christmas coat for our dog! My mother lived out a lovely line of poetry that states, "A woman's love is like a light, shining the brightest in the night."[6]

I know others who also have two professions. One of my friends is a grade-school teacher by day and a gifted tole painter by night. Another is a school principal by day and a writer by night. Another friend is a mother of preschoolers by day and a master oil painter by night.

Again I ask—and urge—you to consider how doing a little night work could help your dreams for your family, for your home, and for some personal creative outlet come true. How can you, like God's beautiful woman, turn a personal passion into a professional line of work? Whisper a prayer to God, the Creator of all things beautiful, and ask Him to guide your heart—and hands—toward a little diligent night work that will help you realize your dreams.

-13-

A Helping Hand
HER MERCY

∽

"She extends her hand to the poor,
Yes, she reaches out her hands to the needy."
Proverbs 31:20

God's beautiful woman is impressive, isn't she?
She excels in trustworthiness, supportiveness,
diligence, industry, thrift, creativity, organization, and micromanagement. But aren't you encouraged to
see that mercy is the next item on the list of her outstanding
qualities? Truly beautiful in God's eyes, the Proverbs 31
woman works hard for her profits, but those profits benefit
people beyond the boundaries of private family life as "she
extends her hand to the poor, yes, she reaches out her hands
to the needy" (Proverbs 31:20). Her efforts and her virtues
benefit her precious family, but she is ever ready to bestow
the soft grace of mercy to the unfortunate. Although she's
busy with her household, she's not so busy that she forgets
the needs of others. Without this godly mercy, her industry
and activity could make her harsh and hurried; she'd be too
busy to care.

Her Hand

For twelve chapters you and I have been marveling at
God's beautiful woman and her strong, energetic body. Now,
Proverbs 31:20 focuses our attention specifically on her hands.

The first part of the verse reads, "She extends her *hand* to the poor." The beauty of God's merciful woman opens up (just like her hand) as we open up the Hebrew language here. The image of the single extended hand reveals her generous, giving nature. For instance, if money is needed, she reaches her hand into her purse and shares her wealth. If bread is lacking, she offers a homemade loaf. If warm clothes are missing, God's merciful and generous woman provides one of her own handmade woolen coats (verse 21), the result of months and months and nights and nights of personal labor (verses 13, 18-19). (In her day, a woolen garment could cost over two months wages![1]) As one woman writes, "I sharpen skills and needles (not my tongue) when neighbors dress in rags and suffer."[2] When it is in her power to do so, the Proverbs 31 woman extends her hand with whatever item is needed (Proverbs 3:27). God's beautiful woman lends a helping hand at every opportunity!

Her Hands

The verse continues: "She [also] reaches out her *hands* to the needy." For the woman who is beautiful in God's eyes, generosity doesn't end with the mere giving of things. The plural word "hands" signifies those activities requiring two hands. Nursing the sick, for instance, requires two hands. So does caring for babies, young children, the elderly, and the sick. The Proverbs 31 woman uses her hands for ministry. She's not afraid to roll up her sleeves and touch those who are suffering. Whatever the need, she holds out her hands—her literal, open, upturned palms—to offer any profits or profitable activities.[3]

Her Heart

It's good to see God's beautiful woman giving, but, as the wise mother and instructor points out to her boy (and to us), this woman's heart is involved. The verbs "extends" and "reaches out" suggest that her giving stretches as far as her means will allow.[4] This kind of stretching, as you know, requires a heart—a generous heart of love and compassion, a heart after God (verse 30). This dear woman gives to the poor and needy with her whole heart.[5]

As she "stretch[es] out" (KJV) her mercy and compassion, she stretches out her heart. Rather than folding her beautiful hands for moments of relaxation, or using them to clutch her profits, or keeping them frantically busy in order to gain greater wealth, she extends her outstretched hands to those around her who are in need! She is aware of these people, sympathetic to their needs, and ready to help, and her full heart and full coffers spill over to liberally and plentifully bless others. Rather than drawing a tight circle around her family and shutting others out, she follows her heart, opens the circle, and takes them in. Her circle of love includes all who need her help.

Her Heeding of God's Word

When I speak, I usually allow some time for questions and answers. For years now, I've kept a handwritten question from one such session. It read, "From your study of Proverbs 31, please comment on the fact that no reference is made to the woman's involvement in 'ministry' kinds of activities."

As I look at God's beautiful woman, I definitely see that one of her ministries is taking care of the poor and the needy (verse 20). Her giving is generated not only from her heart, but out of obedience to and in worship of God. As a woman who fears the Lord (verse 30), she walks in obedience to His Word. And hear now the Word of the Lord on this subject of mercy—and note the blessing God promises:

- "If there is among you a poor man . . . you shall not harden your heart nor shut your hand from your poor brother, but you shall open your hand wide to him and willingly lend him . . . whatever he needs" (Moses' Law, Deuteronomy 15:7-8).

- "He has shown you, O man, what is good; and what does the Lord require of you but to do justly, to love mercy, and to walk humbly with your God" (Micah 6:8).
- "The generous soul will be made rich, and he who waters will also be watered himself " (Proverbs 11:25).
- "He who has pity on the poor lends to the Lord, and He will pay back what he has given" (Proverbs 19:17).
- "He who has a bountiful eye will be blessed, for he gives of his bread to the poor" (Proverbs 22:9).

As we continue to learn what is beautiful in God's eyes, we see that caring for the poor and needy is one of His primary concerns. This beautiful, God-fearing woman knows that fact because she knows God's law and takes His commands seriously. So, I ask you, have you ever considered that perhaps the great blessing upon her home is *because* of her generosity to the poor and needy? That perhaps she is wealthy not because she is a hard worker, a capable manager, or a smart businesswoman, but *because* God blesses her generosity? God's people are God's way of caring for the poor and needy, and He blesses those who care for them in obedience to His Word!

Her Sisters of Mercy

Do you remember when you and I began our climb to the heights of God's beautiful woman? We both found tremendous comfort in the fact that this woman is real, that by God's grace we, too, can attain her level of excellence. Others have also obtained her greatness of character. In her ministry of mercy and giving, God's beautiful woman joins other women in the Bible, fellow sisters of mercy, who live out God's kind of mercy. These beautiful-in-God's-eyes women include Abigail who fed David's 600 men (1 Samuel 25); the starving widow of Zarephath who took in the prophet Elijah (1 Kings 17); the Shunamite woman who regularly fed and lodged the prophet Elisha (2 Kings 4); and Dorcas who clothed the widows in the early church at Joppa (Acts 9). The Proverbs 31 woman is added to this elite list— and you can be, too!

The How-To's of Beauty

Once you begin moving along the gracious path of giving, you'll have no trouble finding golden opportunities to extend God's mercy to the poor and needy. Would some first steps toward becoming a bountiful giver help? Try these for starters.

1. *Begin at home*—Each sunrise presents fresh opportunities for you to show mercy to others, and those opportunities won't go unnoticed. Your children will benefit greatly as they view firsthand the life of a giving mother—a woman who is beautiful in God's eyes.

Edith Schaeffer is such a mother, a woman who extends a helping hand. Regularly the "hobos and tramps" who traveled on the freight cars past her home knocked at her back door asking for a "cup of coffee, ma'am, and maybe some bread?" She never turned one away, but instead she saw each of these men as an opportunity to do something for "one of the least of these" (Matthew 25:40) and perhaps entertain "angels unawares" (Hebrews 13:2). Employing her "hidden art" of hospitality, she toasted nuts, made two generous sandwiches, and heated leftover soup. "For *me*? Is this for me?" was always the bewildered reaction when she stepped through the door from her kitchen holding a tray set with her good china, a bouquet of flowers, a lighted candle—and a copy of the gospel of John to read while he ate and take along with him when he went on his way. Only later did Mrs. Schaeffer discover that her house was marked with chalk—a sign to other tramps that a handout was available. "No matter," Edith smiles. "It was part of our first child Priscilla's education which nothing else could give her!"[6]

2. *Give regularly to your home church*—Most churches minister to the homeless and needy. So through your financial support of your church (1 Corinthians 16:2), you can indirectly lend a helping hand and extend your hand to the poor (Proverbs 31:20). My church stocks a "deacons' closet" for the homeless. Plus a portion of all giving to our church is used to support our missionaries. Your giving to your local church extends in many directions and even around the world.

3. *Keep your ear to the ground*—Take time to notice people around you who are in need. Then purchase double groceries and share them with a struggling couple. Or clean out your wallet when an offering is taken for a special cause. You can also pass your children's clothes on to a young family who's fallen on hard times. When you go to garage sales, pick up needed items that could help others (an aluminum walker for a shut-in, a baby crib for an unwed mother). You can prepare a special meal for a woman undergoing chemotherapy. To reap the many blessings that come with such a ministry of giving, you must keep your ear to the ground. Then these golden opportunities won't pass you by!

4. *Support a worthy organization or person*—Right now I'm studying the women who followed Jesus and supported Him financially (Luke 8:2-3). They set a noble example for you and me because—just as they did—you and I can encourage many individuals and organizations with our financial gifts. You can contribute directly to a mission organization or

support a missionary family you know. You can assist in the training of seminary students by giving to scholarship funds or helping with the purchase of textbooks. You can support young people who are going on a summer missions trip. Why not ask God how you can extend your hands and be involved in His work?

5. *Pray about a personal project*—As you're asking God about where He wants you to be involved in His work in the world, ask Him to direct you to your own personal ministry project which you can support financially. You might be surprised how God answers those prayers—as the following story illustrates.

Sitting in a missions conference, I was personally challenged when I learned how the Central American Mission (CAM) organization began. Two Canadian women, whose husbands owned a coffee plantation in Costa Rica, sat sharing a cup of tea one afternoon in 1879. Deeply concerned for the spiritual needs of the people in that part of the world, and realizing their personal limitations, they began asking God to provide a solution. In February 1891, the first missionary arrived from the United States. Out of the prayers of two women like you and me CAM was born! When you pray, God may touch your generous heart and give you that kind of vision for ministry. Wouldn't that be wonderful?

6. *Err on the side of generosity*—Evangelist Billy Graham smiled proudly as he said this of his wife Ruth: "She manages the fiscal affairs of the household—with . . . more generosity than precision!"[7] How lovely to have a generous heart! You see, like flowing water, money is less useful when it becomes stagnant. You don't want to be like the Dead Sea in Israel, vast and fed with fresh water but useless and dead because the water has no outlet!

Just a caution: If you're married, be sure you work with your husband to set a policy. Find out his views on giving and know where he wants to help out financially. Agree with him and honor his choices. Then set your mind, body, hands, and heart to work on those endeavors.

7. *Live out love*—When asked what love looks like, the early church father Augustine replied, "Love has hands to help others. It has feet to hasten to the poor and needy. It has eyes to see misery and want. It has ears to hear the sighs and sorrow of men. This is what love looks like." What a blessing you are to others as you live out this kind of love. It truly is beautiful in God's eyes!

An Invitation to Beauty

Now, dear one, it's time to evaluate ourselves. It's wonderful to excel in your home, to lead the way in management skills, to perfect your God-given abilities, to shine as a professional, to know that your husband is happy, to keep a tight rein on the family finances, and to watch your savings increase and investments soar. But God highly esteems this great mark of beauty in your life—mercy!

More than any virtue we've looked at so far, mercy reflects the presence of the Lord in your heart and your life. Mercy adds the lovely fragrance of the Lord to who you are and to all you do. Mercy pleases the Lord and is beautiful in His eyes. So I'm praying right now that you will sincerely desire and ask God to help you be a generous, helpful, loving, merciful, truly-beautiful-in-the-Lord woman who delights (and excels!) in giving a helping hand to any and all who are in need. Do it—in the name of the Lord!

-14-

A Double Blessing
HER PREPARATION

Ω

"She is not afraid of snow for her household,
for all her household is clothed with scarlet."
Proverbs 31:21

No one, Jesus proclaimed in His famous Sermon on the Mount, was ever arrayed in clothing as splendid and grand as King Solomon of the Old Testament (Matthew 6:29).

But the family of the Proverbs 31 woman may have come close!

What joy her loved ones stir in her heart—and what joy she brings them as they wear the masterpieces she spins and weaves and decorates. They step out into the bleak streets of Israel clothed like royalty. When her family walks down the street, people can't help but notice!

Now before you start thinking that God's beautiful woman is out of balance here, that she's overly concerned about appearances, that we've found a flaw, and before you write her off as a spendthrift or a clotheshorse, remember something that this godly woman knows to be fact: "Charm is deceitful and beauty is vain" (Proverbs 31:30). Far from being conceited or worldly, God's beautiful woman once again demonstrates her concern and care for other people,

141

her creativity, and her great ability to work. Only this time her efforts are visible to all because now her character expresses itself in her family's clothing.

Looking to the Future

It's a fact! It snows in Israel! I had a hard time imagining this while Jim and I experienced its extreme heat during our studies, as we hiked the dry, barren hills, as we worried more about carrying enough drinking water than about what we wore or how we looked! Even though I have a picture clipped out of the *Los Angeles Times* of devout Jews worshiping at Jerusalem's wailing wall in a foot of snow, I still struggled to imagine snow in Israel.

So I asked our instructor Bill Schlegel, an American who has lived in Israel for thirteen years. "Yes," he heartily nodded, "believe it!" Then he described Jerusalem's wet, cold, windy winters that people endure in their frigid stone buildings, on stone streets, and behind stone walls and with little or no heat. Bill himself went without heat one winter for two months, and that winter it snowed 15 inches—twice! Despite the unrelenting heat I experienced, one can count on snow almost annually in Palestine.

God's beautiful woman knows that snow comes to her homeland, but "she is not afraid of snow for her household" (Proverbs 31:21). Why? Because she's prepared for the future, whatever it will hold. Ever looking ahead, she wisely provides for her family. "All her household is clothed with scarlet," verse 21 concludes.

Now this foresight and her proactive efforts shouldn't be a surprise to us. For thirteen chapters we've seen the Proverbs 31 woman's great heart of love, her wisdom, her willingness, her ability to plan ahead, and her management tactics. We know that she's a planner who is always looking to the future and planning for it (verses 15 and 27). I can easily imagine that, long before a single snowflake even thought of forming, a scene like this occurred:

Rising early one morning (verse 15), this oh-so-beautiful-in-God's-eye's woman turns her prayer concerns to her dear family. As she lifts each of them to God in prayer and considers ways to express her love to them, she grabs her "to do" list and jots several notes to herself: "Prepare for winter. Get wool. Locate some red dye. Spin yarn. Weave fabric. Make winter coats." She will bless her family with the winter clothing they need!

"Extended Care" Living

But notice just who is fortunate enough to be blessed in this way. The verse says, "*All* her household is clothed with scarlet" (Proverbs 31:21). Everyone who lives under this beautiful woman's roof is handsomely and warmly clothed with scarlet cloaks of wool for winter.

You see, the Proverbs 31 woman takes care of everyone. That's why I'm calling her kind of care "extended care"! We've seen in verse 20 her care extended to the poor and afflicted. Whether the need is food or clothing, nursing assistance or help cleaning a house, she offers it.

But God's beautiful woman also extends her care to her extended family. Consider who would be living under her roof. We've met her husband and heard that there are children. Also in her day (and for many of us, too) elderly parents are a part of the household. Married children—and their children—are probably there. So are orphaned nieces and nephews and widowed relations. And, oh yes, the servants (verse 15)! Quite a group depends on her provision, and she provides generously. "All her household is clothed with scarlet!"

Clothes Fit for a King

And what does it mean that God's beautiful woman clothes her family members in "scarlet"? The color reveals much about her provision.

- *Warmth*—Red, or scarlet (meaning "to shine"), indicates the retention of heat.[1]

- *Stately appearance*—Scarlet is the color of kings' clothing[2] and signifies dignity,[3] luxury, and magnificence.[4]

- *Quality*—Only the best will do for this beautiful woman's family. The fact that they are clothed with wool—and with scarlet wool at that!—speaks of the quality clothing she provides. Then, as well as now, very few people owned more than one woolen overcoat.

- *Double thickness*—I'm sure you've felt the difference between cheap, thin wool and that which is rich and heavy. Well, one meaning of the Hebrew word for scarlet is "double," and of course God's beautiful woman would only make quality, double-thick clothing, extending a double blessing to her brood.

- *Double dipped*—Wool has to be dyed the color scarlet, and to become truly scarlet, wool was dipped into the dye more than once.

- *Costly*—Because of the dye and the added labor and time, scarlet robes were luxurious and costly.[5]

It's amazing that the mere mention of scarlet clothing reveals so much about the heart of the seamstress and conveys such a powerful message from that heart to the heart of those for whom she sews!

The How-To's of Beauty

Even more amazing is that you and I are able to send the same powerful message of love. Our family members will be blessed when we care enough to prepare and provide for their future needs. Just as God's beautiful woman, armed with her calendar and a "to do" list, takes the time to anticipate her family's future needs and prepare for them, so can you. Here are a few items to put at the top of your "to do" list.

1. Determine future needs—Lay out a one-year calendar and determine your future needs. Think about the maintenance work you need done inside your home—winterizing, summerizing, or cleaning the upholstery, drapes, and carpets. Wool clothes need to be moth-proofed and stored. Firewood needs to be ordered.

Next, think through your outdoor responsibilities. Do you have a swimming pool to be emptied, roses to be pruned back, or gutters to be cleared out? When do you need to prepare your garden, plant your seeds, and bury your bulbs?

And which special family occasions are coming up? Is someone graduating, getting married, or having a baby? Have you marked all the birthdays and anniversaries on your calendar? You already know you have Thanksgiving and Christmas and Easter—and vacations—to prepare for! And the list goes on with back-to-school preparations, open houses, special guests for dinner, family reunions, etc.

Mark every anticipated future event and need on your calendar. Your goal is, just as it is for God's beautiful woman, to be far-sighted, to look forward through your eyes of love and, acting in wisdom, prepare!

2. Prepare for emergencies—This item was slow in making sense to me, but after the 6.8 earthquake my family went through in Southern California in 1994, it tops my list!

Caught without a single flashlight, we now have one in every room . . . and purse . . . and drawer . . . and suitcase . . . and car. And I never leave home without one!

But this call to preparedness applies to everyone everywhere, not just to others living in earthquake country. My parents lived in tornado country—and they were prepared. My daughter Courtney lived in Kauai where there are hurricanes. Do you live in a picturesque snowy region—where there might be avalanches? Or along a beautiful river bank—that may flood with too much rain?

Let me repeat myself: Everyone everywhere needs to prepare for emergencies. Each of us needs to practice fire drills, determine emergency plans, and gather first-aid supplies, emergency food, and water. God's beautiful woman is "not afraid" (verse 21) because she is *prepared*, and—with a little preparation—you can enjoy that same peace of mind.

3. *Care for the clothing*—Top on the list when it comes to caring for your family's clothes is keeping the clothes clean. So pick a day to be wash day, and don't forget—this one is hard for me!—the laundry isn't done until it's washed, dried, folded, pressed, *and* put away! Your goal is to provide clothes that are ready to wear, and that means sewing on those loose or missing buttons. Also see that clothes are protected—moth-proofed, stored, and covered—when necessary. The dollar value of your clothes adds up. Just ask your insurance agent! In the day of the Proverbs 31 woman, clothes were actually used as money for deposits and trade (Proverbs 20:16).

4. *Consider quality*—Just as the Marines only need "a few good men," your family only needs a few good clothes. It's obvious (by the scarlet color) that God's beautiful woman concerns herself with providing quality clothes for her family—not quantity!

5. *Consider comfort*—The comfort, protection, warmth, and health of your family is undoubtedly a major concern for you, and that's a concern that God's beautiful woman shares. In fact, there's no doubt that her concern for her family's comfort is the motivation behind the scarlet garments. The clothing is red, of double thickness, and of high quality for a reason: Such a coat would be warm as well as beautiful—a double blessing!

6. *Consider beauty*—The woman who is beautiful in God's eyes models His standards for us in all of her life, including how she provides clothing for her family. Since she is a professional weaver and artist, wouldn't you imagine that the clothes she provides for her household are beautiful? Obviously they were colorful and fine, intricately woven with beads, jewels, and gold thread (Proverbs 31:21,22,24). But knowing the virtues of the Proverbs 31 woman, I'm confident that her expression of beauty is never overdone. The clothes she makes are simply another expression of her great love—which you can express to your family, too, straight from your own beautiful heart.

Now, dear reader, I simply can't leave this subject without telling you about my friend LaTonya, a mother of five girls. It makes my day when I see her with her smiling husband and those five darling daughters all dressed up on Sunday morning. I can't imagine the time it takes LaTonya to braid, ribbon, and barrette all the little pigtails, ponytails, and hairdos! From their polished little patent-leather shoes to their starched-and-ironed dresses, from their scrubbed-until-they-shine faces and glistening hair to their tiny purses and Bibles, they are little testimonies to LaTonya's loving care. Her family is truly blessed by her devotion to provide for them—and yours will be, too!

An Invitation to Beauty

At first glance a chapter on clothing and preparation doesn't look terribly important, does it? But, dear one, this chapter is about yet another virtue this woman who is beautiful in God's eyes possesses. It's about preparation.

First of all, know that the work of preparation is important to God and that He will guide your planning. After all, He provides for us. His very name is "Jehovah-jireh, God will provide"! You and I mirror this aspect of His character when we provide for our loved ones, and our provision happens more easily—if not more bountifully—when we plan and prepare. Second, when we work to provide clothing for our family and when we prepare for their future needs, our actions speak forth a loud message of love. Then, having prepared for the seasons of life and having placed your trust in our caring, loving, gracious, all-sufficient God, there is never a place in your home for fear. Blessed by your preparations *and* by God's provision, your loved ones are indeed doubly blessed!

-15-

A Tapestry of Beauty
HER HANDIWORK

"She makes herself coverings of tapestry;
her clothing is silk and purple."
Proverbs 31:22 (KJV)

*B*efore you and I catch our first—and only!—glimpse of the woman who is beautiful in God's eyes actually doing something for herself, I want us to pause and look back at the path we've been traveling. Since we began our climb in the first chapter (remember Masada?), we've taken step after step toward God's kind of beauty, guided along by His lovely Proverbs 31 woman.

We've seen in the wonder of her character that God's beautiful woman is truly a person of virtue and excellence. We've seen how her strength of mind and body enables her to handle well the challenges and demands of daily life. We've marveled at her constant, deep love for her husband and children, a love which she lives out in her actions. She finds no sacrifice for them too costly. And far from stopping at her doorpost, her love extends beyond her family to the needy in her household and community. We have no doubt about her capable management, her creativity, or her awesome diligence.

As I mentioned earlier, mere survival was the paramount issue for people of the Old Testament as each new day dawned in their destitute land. But we've seen this woman, who is an army of virtues, not only provide the essentials of existence, but provide abundantly—so much so that she has enough to give to the poor and some to sell to those who can afford it! Now, with the basics of food and clothing for her family taken care of, she turns her attention to decorating her home. We are allowed to peek into the home of God's beautiful woman and even catch a glimpse of her. But I don't want to race ahead of our text. First her beautiful home!

House Beautiful

What woman doesn't delight in making her home a place of beauty? And God's beautiful woman is no different. In fact she surpasses them all (Proverbs 31:29)!

Proverbs 31:22 says, "She makes herself coverings of tapestry." At first glance this sentence seems to be describing her wardrobe, but the "coverings of tapestry" are actually her home furnishings. Some translators of the Bible call these furnishings carpets, woven coverlets, and upholstery.[1] One version even says, "She makes her own quilts"![2]

As we've seen, weaving plays an important role in the life of God's beautiful woman and in her Middle Eastern culture. A creative artist with an end product in mind, she gathers wool and flax and then works the raw materials into a usable state. Spending many late night hours with her distaff and spindle, she spins her wool and flax into yarn and thread, weaves it into fantastic fabrics only an artist could envision, and uses it to clothe her family—in the red of royalty, clothing fit for kings! But she has leftover yarn, fabric, creativity, and energy! So why not make tapestries of beauty for the home, tapestries also fit for kings?

So, with busy hands and an overflowing heart of love, God's beautiful woman sets about making tapestry for pillows, blankets, cushions, drapes, rugs, wall hangings, tablecloths, runners, mats, and upholstery to adorn her home. Our beautiful weaver also designs and makes napkins, hand towels, sheets, quilts, coverlets, and bedspreads. A variety of colors, textures, patterns, and styles adds beauty and warmth to her stone house, transforming it into a delight for the senses. She truly is an artist! Each object of her handiwork is a masterpiece!

This fact is supported by an image hidden in the wording of verse 22 and created by the word *makes* ("she *makes* herself coverings of tapestry"). Our Proverbs 31 woman makes the tapestry in the basic sense: She uses her hands to do this hard work. But *makes* also means "spreads" or "decks." The Hebrew language paints a picture of an enticing bed of comfort and luxury.[3] When God's beautiful woman is finished, her bed is "spread" with colorfully woven pillows, mattresses, coverlets, and tapestry.[4] Indeed, her entire home is "decked out," a rich tapestry of beauty!

Beauty Check

Before we leave the Proverbs 31 woman's house and home, let's take a look around our own home at the tapestry of beauty we're weaving for our House Beautiful.

Check #1: Pretend you're a visitor—Walk through the place where you live. What do you see? What would a guest notice? What mood does your home invite? What pleases you about what you see—and what would you like to improve? Any eyesores? Clutter? As the homemaker—the maker of your home—you are in the position to generate powerful impressions and create a welcoming atmosphere and beautiful environment.

Check #2: Plan several home improvements—God's beautiful woman is certainly a do-it-yourselfer! Keep that in mind as you take inventory of your home. What projects are you working on? Right now I'm hunting for some red paisley sheets to make into curtains for my office window. Do your cabinets need a fresh coat of stain or polish? Are there grease spots on your carpet you could remove with a little elbow grease? Do your windows need a good cleaning? What repairs have you been putting off?

Not all home improvements cost money. In fact, the greatest improvement of all can be cleaning up and removing clutter! (I'll be cleaning out my bedroom closet when this book is done! I'm terribly convicted just writing about clutter!) Some of the most dramatic improvements come from your heart and mind. I'm talking about putting a single flower in a bud vase, displaying an item of color or interest, rearranging furniture, adding knickknacks to the coffee tables, and using some personal treasures to add your caring touch and unique flair to your decor.

Check #3: Pass it by your husband—God's beautiful woman has her priorities in order. The first item on her list is clothing for her family. After that comes the house. Be sure—with your husband and your checkbook—that now is the right time to spend money on home decor. After all, God's beautiful woman knows how to wait (Proverbs 19:2).

Check #4: Put in some overtime—And I mean put in some overtime at home, not at the office. God's beautiful woman works long and late (Proverbs 31:18). So set aside a Saturday or an evening or two for a home-improvement project.

Wherever home is for you, it's an expression of *you*—*your* virtues, *your* abilities, *your* love. You may not be able to determine the kind of home you have, but you can determine its beauty. You control whether it's clean, organized, and orderly. You also choose your favorite colors, styles, and moods.

But maybe your home is hardly ideal. Well, consider some of the places your sisters in the Bible called home! Eve cared for a garden. Mrs. Noah managed an ark. Sarah was queen of a tent. Esther lived in a palace in a foreign land. Mary spent time in a stable. Peter's mother-in-law offered the gift of hospitality in her stone dwelling. So no matter how often the place you live changes, *you* are the beautiful woman with the beautiful heart who turns it into a home. *You* are in charge of the handiwork and decorations that make your residence a "Home, Sweet Home"!

I faced a real homemaking challenge when our family served as missionaries in Singapore. Over there, both the houses we lived in were concrete—walls, floors, and ceilings. (In fact, when we cleaned the house, we just turned on the hose and hosed it down and out!) There on the equator, far away from all my family and friends, I nevertheless "built" my home, giving it all the touches of warmth and love I could (Proverbs 14:1). Then, returning to the United States, we faced more challenges as we moved four times in two months, sleeping in sleeping bags on the floor in two of those places. But each place was home because I was determined to make it one! Even four sleeping bags lying in a row can be beautiful in a place you're making home!

A Touch of Class

At last! Everyone has been well taken care of. Those in need are warm. The family members are striking in their garments of red. The house is beautiful and able to minister love and peace to all who pass through its doorway. Now it is time for God's beautiful woman to think about what she herself will wear. It's time for her to put on the ornaments suited to her station and means.

First we see that "her clothing is silk and purple" (Proverbs 31:22). Ever the artist and a grand lady, she gives her clothing a touch of class. God's beautiful woman deserves silk and purple—and it becomes her! As a woman of virtue, wisdom, strength, and dignity, she is precisely the caliber of woman who should wear such regal clothing. Her clothing is simply a reflection of her character.

Although Proverbs reports that her clothing is made of silk, that word is better understood as fine linen, the fabric she weaves from her flax. Elegance has emerged as she has sewn, and now, when touched by the sun, the fine white linen glistens like silk. What she fashions for herself to wear reveals her inner clothing of "strength and dignity" (verse 25).

We also learn that her clothes are purple, colored by a rare and costly dye extracted in minute quantities from a shellfish found on the eastern shores of the Mediterranean Sea.[5] God's beautiful woman probably exchanged her handiwork for this rare, expensive dye when the merchant ships came in. The purple is clearly another indication of her hard work and shrewd management.

A Touch of Taste

All this talk of expense and exquisiteness may sound proud or showy or frivolous, but we need to keep in mind a few facts.

First of all, God's beautiful woman does not have a closet full of clothes. She has a few quality items, each of which took her months (maybe even a year) to make for herself.

Second, Proverbs 31 is a poem of praise. Along with her many virtues, she is praised for the beauty of her wardrobe. Her clothes are cut from fantastically woven handmade fabrics, they are adorned with detailed needlework, and they are warm, rich, and regal in color—and she does all this herself, starting with raw flax and wool (verse 13) and ending with splendid garments.

Also don't forget that God's beautiful woman never forgets her priorities. She would never slight others in order to parade in finery. Such selfishness would be neither praiseworthy nor beautiful! She rightly places herself last.

Finally, remember that these words of Proverbs 31 are the words of another noble woman. And who knows a woman better than another woman? King Lemuel's mother makes a special point of telling him how the woman of his dreams should be dressed. This knowing mother focuses on:

- The *position* in society which God's beautiful woman holds—She is a woman of dignity, wealth, and high ranking, and her clothing is suitable to her station.

- Her *practice* of hard work and skillful management which pays off in practical ways—She has the finances and is willing to invest the time and effort to dress according to her position.

- Her *professional status*—As she sails along the cobblestone passages that crisscross Jerusalem, she is a walking advertisement for her skillful handiwork. A seamstress certainly should not dress shabbily!

- Her *praiseworthy character*—The virtuous wife is robed in what speaks of her true character and dignity.

With this perspective in mind, we gladly join with the young prince's mother as she exults, "Give her of the fruit of her hands, and let her own works praise her in the gates" (Proverbs 31:31)! This woman who is altogether beautiful in God's eyes is fully deserving of her finery.

The How-To's of Beauty

Considering what God is saying to us in Proverbs 31:22 about our personal wardrobe, I believe His message comes down to three main ideas.

1. Your care—Taking care of your clothes is as important as the clothes themselves. Your level of care shows up in the mending of a tear, the sewing-on of a button, the removal of a spot, the washing of dirty clothes, and (don't forget that most important final step) the ironing-out of wrinkles and the ironing-in of creases! The way you care for your clothes reveals something of your character and what you value. So consider the general condition and overall appearance of your clothes. What message might the way you take care of your clothes be sending? Beauty begins with cleanliness and neatness.

2. Your reflection—You're not the only person affected by your appearance. How you dress and how you look also sends a message about your family. When you maintain a certain level of cleanliness and dignity in public, you can be a positive reflection on your husband and his name, his reputation, and his (and your!) children.

The husband of God's beautiful woman "is known in the gates" (verse 23), but not as the poor man who's married to a slob or the man whose wife is a mess. (As one clever author notes, "MRS. in front of your name does not mean *miserable rut of sloppiness!*"[6]) No, the husband of the Proverbs 31 woman is known in the gates as the man who is married to a *lady*, a meticulous, gracious, attractive woman of character.

And it's no different for you or me! How we look is a direct reflection on our husband and our children—and even our parents and the company we work for! Other people can form their opinions of your entire family based on their perception of you, which can be based on how you look. That being the case, I try to follow this bit of advice: "Be different, if it means being cleaner, neater, and better groomed than the group. It is always better to arrive for any function looking slightly better, rather than slightly worse than the others."[7]

3. *Your standards*—As women seeking the kind of beauty God highly esteems, you and I want to follow His standards. And exactly what are those standards? *Modesty* heads His list, which continues with *soberness* (meaning acting or dressing in a proper and sensible manner), *moderation, discretion,* and *chasteness* (see 1 Timothy 2:9 and Titus 2:5). These words may sound old-fashioned, but these qualities flow out of a heart intent on godliness (1 Timothy 2:10). And our loving Lord is always more concerned about the clothing of your heart than He is with how you clothe your external, outer, physical body: "Do not let your beauty be that outward adorning of arranging the hair, of wearing gold, or of putting on fine apparel; but let it be the hidden person of the heart, with the incorruptible ornament of a gentle and quiet spirit, which is very precious in the sight of God" (1 Peter 3:3-4). Amen!

An Invitation to Beauty

Now it's your turn to express yourself creatively in the beauty of your home and your clothing. Everything in its time!

The Proverbs 31 woman who is beautiful in God's eyes is a weaver, but you are a weaver, too. You can weave your own tapestry of beauty right in your own home—wherever home is! What will you need? In a word, love. With threads of love woven by hands of love and expressing a heart of love, you can creatively transform even a camper into a home. That transformation occurs anywhere and anytime your heart and handiwork come together.

Know then, dear weaver of beauty, that God has given us opportunity upon opportunity to not only express our love but to be creative as we share that love. Your decorations of both home and wardrobe can bless so many by their beauty. We read in the psalms that "the heavens declare the glory of God; and the firmament shows His handiwork" (Psalm 19:1). On a smaller scale, your handiwork can also bring glory to God *and* show forth something of His beauty. So set your heart in motion, your mind to spinning, and your fingers to work and see what handiwork you can generate to glorify your wonderful God!

-16-

A Man of Influence
HER HUSBAND

∾

"Her husband is known in the gates,
when he sits among the elders of the land."
Proverbs 31:23

*A*lthough our culture may not value it, one of the wife's most important roles is to support her husband. A woman who is beautiful in God's eyes knows how to do just that. Let me give you the example of Susannah Spurgeon, the wife of Charles Spurgeon, famed preacher at London's Metropolitan Tabernacle. His ministry was thriving, but he became concerned that he might be neglecting his children, so Charles Spurgeon returned home earlier than usual one evening. Opening the door, he was surprised to find no children in the hall. Ascending the stairs, he heard his wife's voice and knew that she was engaged in prayer with the children. She named each of the children in prayer. When she finished her prayer and her nightly instructions to their little ones, Spurgeon thought, "I can go on with my work. My children are well cared for."[1] Imagine! Because of her faithfulness and diligence at home, Mrs. Spurgeon gave the world Charles Haddon Spurgeon, his words which continue to stir and convict hearts today, and their two sons, who also became ministers.

Marriage to a Man of Influence

At this point of Proverbs 31, we finally learn something about the husband of God's beautiful woman! You and I were introduced to him in verse 11 as a trusting husband who rests his soul safely upon the character of his beautiful-in-God's-eyes wife. He's the fortunate man she is committed to doing good to all the days of her life (verse 12). We've witnessed the meals she prepares for him (verse 15), as well as her management of his home (verse 15) and finances (verse 11). And, thanks to her handiwork, he is splendidly clothed in scarlet (verse 21). "Who can find a virtuous wife (verse 10)?" Well, this man has! God has definitely graced him with one of His truly beautiful women!

In addition to being richly blessed by God through his wife, this man is himself a blessing to many. You see, he is a man of influence. Let me explain.

"Her husband is known in the gates, when he sits among the elders of the land" (Proverbs 31:23). In the days of the Proverbs 31 woman, cities were walled around for protection, but gates allowed for entrance and exit. These gated entrances contained one or more large rooms built into the city wall. In fact, whenever Jim and I visited any sizable city, we saw evidence of the thick stone walls that once protected it and the many spacious chambered gates. Some of these compartments were set aside as guard rooms, complete with a well for water, a place for a fire, and inside steps leading up to the top of the wall. Other chambers served as official government offices.

And exactly what happened in the gates as the townspeople passed through them in their daily comings and goings? In the coolness and protection of these stone rooms, legal and governmental decisions were made. Deliberations took place. Political issues were settled. Official proclamations and edicts were read. Matters of public welfare were transacted. Judgments were administered. Legal questions were decided.

This is the place where the husband of the Proverbs 31 woman is "known" (verse 23). In fact, known to be a reputable man, he "sits among the elders of the land." Clearly, he makes a notable contribution to public life. Recognized as a leader, he is in a position to influence the life of the community. He may even have had a seat in the gate, signifying his status as a man of importance and an able counselor. He may have been one of the elders, the judicial body which ruled the land. This prestigious group met daily in the town gate to transact any public business or decide cases that were brought before them.[2] Whatever the specific situation, we see that this man is well known because he sits in the council chambers with other respected civic leaders who are conducting legal business.[3] An honored citizen, he is held in high esteem by the townspeople and the officials of his community and, therefore, is truly a man of influence.

Behind Every Good Man

Do you remember the setting for the teaching of Proverbs 31:10-31? A young prince—a leader in the making, a king to be, a ruler in process, a future man of influence—is learning the ABCs of life (Proverbs 31:1). His wise and beautiful-in-God's-eyes mother is herself married to a leader, a king, a ruler, a man of influence. So, faithful, passionate teacher that she is, she has been describing for her young son the kind of wife a man of influence needs. So far we've seen that this woman must be fit for a king, as powerful and effective in her realm as he will be in his, and, like him, earning the respect and esteem of the community as she serves. Clearly, God's wise mother knows that behind every good man stands a good woman! (As a more modern "proverb" puts it, "Generally, when a man climbs the ladder to success, his wife is holding the ladder!")

As I think about the husband and wife pictured in Proverbs 31, I think of them as a pair of bookends. Both of them are pillars in the community, both are known in the gates (verses 23 and 31), and both are committed to the good of others (verses 20 and 23). Although their spheres of influence are different, they both exhibit the same virtuous character as they live with the same purpose, that of serving others. Just as wise Solomon noted, "Two are better than one" (Ecclesiastes 4:9). As evidence, consider how this matched set works together.

- He contributes to the community; she is his helpmeet (Genesis 2:18).
- He is successful in the realm of city management; she is successful in the realm of family and home management.
- He is happy at work; she is happy working at home.
- He is respected and held in high esteem; she preserves and advances his honor by her conduct and example.
- He is deferred to as a solid, influential citizen; she brings credit to him.
- He is a counselor, a man of common sense and not-so-common insight; she speaks with loving wisdom.
- He exerts his influence on the life of the community in the city gates; she influences the community from home.
- He is known for his solid character and important contributions; so is she.
- He has achieved some worldly wealth and social status; she improves his financial situation as well as his social standing by what she is to him and what she does for him as a wife.
- He has reached his professional aims; she has helped him do so by her diligence and frugality.

- He has earned prestige; she is respected for her creative handiwork.
- He is a virtuous man; she is a virtuous woman.
- He is crowned with honor; she is his crown (Proverbs 12:4).

A Woman of Influence

Oh, my dear friend, it's vital that you and I understand the inestimable contribution we can make to our husband as he pursues his career and serves the Lord in his job. First consider how this man of influence is his wife's gift to the people. He's out there in public. He leaves home daily, following God's plan for his life and making a difference in the community, if not the world!

Behind him, however, stands this wonderful, beautiful woman. One reason he can succeed and thrive in his position of influence is the fact that he has no worries at home. In fact, his honorable and prosperous home enhances his reputation. By virtue of his *wife's* character and *her* ability to manage the home, *he* is able to serve in his position of influence. *She* enables *him* to sit in the gate among the elders of the land. The well-ordered home which *she* runs reflects positively on her husband as *he* has risen in worldly wealth and social power. Furthermore, *her* diligence and thriftiness at home have enabled *him* to dream his dreams and reach them. The influence our beautiful woman has had on her husband has clearly helped him become a man of influence in the community.

Now I want to ask you whether you see your husband's service "out there" as your gift to the people he serves. After all, *you* are the one who fills him up and sends him off to be a blessing to others. He is *your* contribution to society, to the company he works for, to the people in his office, to his customers, to his students, to his flock—whatever the case may be.

And he is your contribution whether you hold down a job or spend every waking minute at home. You support him not because you may or may not earn a paycheck yourself. Your support is a matter of your heart and your home; the issue is how you take care of him, his home, and his children. It's about your beautiful contribution to his well-being.

The How-To's of Beauty

Exactly how do you and I make that valuable contribution? How do we support our husband and beautify his life? Here are some ideas.

1. Praise him—Every human being appreciates words of sincere praise, and your husband is no different. So, as Proverbs 3:27 says, "Do not withhold good from those to whom it is due, when it is in the power of your hand to do so." It is definitely in the power of your hand—and heart and mouth!—to praise your man, so do so today and every day of your life (Proverbs 31:12). As someone has quipped, "He can't read it on his tombstone when he's dead!"

2. Encourage him—Every human being—including your dear husband—also needs encouragement. Correction can help, but encouragement can help far more, as an unidentified husband realized. Marveling about his wife, he wrote, "You see some hidden, struggling trait, encourage it and make it great!" Proverbs 12:25 says, "A good word makes the heart glad," and a good word from you gives your husband courage to face life's challenges. So open that beautiful mouth and speak words of wisdom and kindness. Let love and encouragement flow (Proverbs 31:26).

3. Take care of your marriage—The truth isn't very romantic, but in case you haven't noticed, marriage is work! Martin Luther observed, "Marriage is not a joke. It must be worked on, and prayed over."[4] As a wife, you are called to pray for your husband and to respect him (Ephesians 5:33). The Amplified Bible explains it this way: "Let the wife see that she respects and reverences her husband—that she notices him, regards him, honors him, prefers him, venerates and esteems him; and that she defers to him, praises him, and loves and admires him exceedingly."[5] This is a tall order, an order for a lifetime! But if you follow through on this calling from God, you'll be a beautiful wife—and a wife who enjoys a beautiful marriage.

4. *Take care of your family*—The husband of the Proverbs 31 woman is a man of influence on his job and in his community because his wife is a woman of influence in the home. And here's another calling from God—and another of His standards of beauty: You are to take care of your family. You are to take seriously the meals, the schedule, the clothing, the counsel and training you give the children. By running his home smoothly and effectively, you contribute to both your husband's public reputation and his usefulness in the church (see 1 Timothy 3:4-5). Nothing credits a man as much as a beautiful-in-God's-eyes wife and a beautifully behaved family!

5. *Take care of your home*—Be sure all is well at home. Tap into God's great grace for help to handle the daily drudgeries and even the unexpected challenges of life. Ask the Lord to help you delight in watching over the ways of your household (verse 27).

6. *Take care of your finances*—Your wise money management is a gift to your husband. It buys him some financial freedom to follow his abilities and his heart into an occupation of choice rather than necessity. By keeping watch over your family day by day, by holding down the spending,

upping the savings, and increasing the earnings, you follow in the footsteps of God's wise and beautiful woman.

7. *Let him go*—When Jim first began serving on our church's pastoral staff, I struggled to get used to his absences, his late hours, and his seven-day-a-week calling. The following words from a wife's prayer of relinquishment showed me a better way to support and serve Jim; they helped me to let Jim go.

> God . . . I declare afresh that my husband belongs to You, not to me. I have yielded all right to him—all right to his time, his understanding, his attention, his love. I will take what You give back as privileges to be used for my enjoyment and for Your glory as long as You see fit to give these privileges to us.
>
> I purpose to refuse [to let] any thoughts of self-pity, criticism, jealousy, or resentment creep in when these precious privileges are denied—when his time is taken up by others . . . when he seems to have failed in consideration and love.
>
> Lord . . . help Yourself to my husband's life to spend it however You choose to let him spend it, regardless of the disadvantages to me personally.[6]

These words express a significantly more beautiful attitude than clinging, whining, complaining, nagging, and begrudging your husband the time he needs to do what he needs to do.

8. *Support his dreams*—A pastor's wife I greatly admire helped me tremendously when Jim entered seminary to prepare for a life of ministry. When I asked for her Number One piece of advice for a struggling seminary wife, she responded with a four-page letter. Her wise advice included the fol-

lowing: "Dream with your husband about the effect of his ministry. Share in the expectation and excitement together. Later on the goals you establish will issue from 'the dream.' It will carry you during dry and trying times and help you remain faithful to the Lord, always seeking His best. 'The dream' keeps your focus on our great God and not on the day-to-day situations."

These words express a heart attitude that must indeed be beautiful in God's eyes. So, whatever your husband's job, his place of employment, his sphere of influence, pour your strength into him by supporting rather than ignoring, belittling, or even laughing at his dreams.

9. *Realize that your behavior is a reflection on him*—The husband of the Proverbs 31 woman "is known in the gates" (verse 23) for, among other things, having a worthy wife! Is that one of the reasons your husband is known and respected?

An Invitation to Beauty

Isn't Proverbs 31:23 a beautiful and empowering verse of Scripture? If you're married, I hope you are realizing that you and your husband are not two separate entities pursuing two separate causes in two separate directions. No, you are like a pair of bookends. You stand together as a unit, facing together and managing together all the facets and challenges, all the causes and concerns, all the opportunities and dreams that make up your life together. Rejoice that you are equal in influence and contribution, although you live out that influence and contribution in separate arenas. Rejoice when your husband is the center of attention, when he excels, when he is recognized and honored. Rejoice in the privilege of following Jesus' footsteps and giving your life for your husband in sacrificial love, making the supreme sacrifice of your self for him.

As you face this challenge, I invite you to pray and ask God to help you support your husband in ways that will strengthen him and glorify God. Make a Proverbs 31:12 commitment to do your husband good all the days of your life by praising him, encouraging him, nurturing your marriage, serving your family, tending to your home, watching over the finances, supporting his dreams, and praying for his success— that he may be a man of godly influence in his work and his community.

-17-

A Creative Professional
HER INDUSTRY

⌒

"She makes linen garments and sells them,
and supplies sashes for the merchants."
Proverbs 31:24

I love hearing the success stories of artists and entrepreneurs. (In fact, I have folders full of these remarkable tales!) Whenever I hear about a woman our society labels "successful," I wonder, "How did it happen? What steps did she take? Where did her knowledge and skills come from?" Amazingly, as each woman's story unfolds, two common essentials for success emerge: She developed *something personal* into *something professional*.

As I write this chapter, I can think of many women who fit this description of success. They are accomplished, energetic, ever-learning. And best of all, they are dedicated to teaching women like you and me the skills for homemaking, decorating, food preparation, crafts, gift making, gardening, and scrapbooking. These wonderful women love their homes and love being busy and creative. And they want to show others how to do the same and experience the same joy and fulfillment.

When I think of women like this, I can't help but recall God's assignment to His women to be "teachers of good things" (Titus 2:3). I know I am greatly blessed to have grown

169

up in the Lord and in the church in the shadow of an army of these industrious women who actively pass on what they know.

Whatever skills and talents God has given to you, and whatever knowledge you possess that has turned *something personal* into *something professional*, I hope you will take every opportunity to better the lives of others. I pray that you will dedicate yourself to heeding God's assignment to you to fill others with the "good things" that you know and they yearn to know!

You and I may never take our skills to a business or professional level, but each of us can set our hearts on creating beauty in our homes for those who enter. Like God's beautiful Proverbs 31 woman, we can develop an eye and a heart for beauty. Our homes provide the perfect soil for the joyous creativity that will result. In fact, you and I can nurture our own creative enterprises right there and right now by giving our wholehearted attention to our daily work at home (something personal). With the joy of the Lord as our strength (Nehemiah 8:10), we can transform our daily work into enduring works of art.

The Birth of a Business

Just as the pattern in a piece of wood repeats itself in cut after cut, so weaving is ingrained in the soul of the Proverbs 31 woman. It's definitely her "thing"! Just look at the number of times the little prince's mother mentions our beautiful woman's weaving: she seeks wool and flax for her fabrics (verse 13); she sits up late processing her raw materials by candlelight (verses 18-19); she gives her warm handmade garments to the poor (verse 20); and she regally decks out her family, her home, and herself with her handiwork (verses 21-22).

Now young King Lemuel's mother points once again to the dignity and beauty of the Proverbs 31 woman's skills as a weaver: "She makes linen garments and sells them, and supplies sashes for the merchants" (verse 24).

Moving systematically through this poem of praise, you and I have watched this woman who is so beautiful in God's eyes expand her sphere of influence and industry. Now we realize that her efforts have overflowed the banks of hearth and home and crossed over the boundaries of community. She has created a full-fledged industry that reaches to the markets of the known world. Her handiwork—originally created at home from a heart of love for those near and dear to her—is now at the heart of a thriving business. The beautiful work of her hands is carried by merchant ships and camel caravans to the ends of the earth. In case you were bothered by her not being a "career woman," you can see that she is—and is she ever! The selling of her items to foreign markets speaks of the quality of her work, explains her prosperity, and proves that she is a creative professional.[1] Something personal became something professional!

The Expression of Creativity

Clearly, in the case of God's beautiful woman, her God-given creativity plus the desire to better her family finances added up to a profession. Something personal (her ability and her desires for her family) became something professional (her cottage industry).

And it all began with an outlet for her creativity: "She makes linen garments" (Proverbs 31:24). First she made the linen fabric itself, and then she made the clothes from it. The fineness of her linen made it soft and usable for bedclothes, undergarments, or lightweight tunic-like smocks worn in the summer on a bare body. Her linen garments were thin and fine—and therefore costly!

This beautiful woman's handiwork also includes sashes, and we see that she "supplies sashes for the merchants" (verse 24). Like a belt or girdle, a sash was worn to gather the flowing garments (still worn in Israel today) so that movement was easier. Leather belts were common, but a linen sash or belt was more attractive and more costly, woven with gold and silver thread and studded with jewels and gold. These were the works of art she "supplies . . . for the merchants."

The Enrichment of Estate

For the Proverbs 31 woman a business was born when something personal to her became something professional. Her business grew out of her personal creativity *and* her personal desire to enrich her estate. So "she makes linen garments and *sells* them" (verse 24). God's beautiful woman merchandises her goods, producing them for the specific purpose of economic trade. Intent on improving her family's financial situation and knowing that her merchandise is good (verse 18), she moves her handmade goods out from the home and into the local markets.

The sashes she supplies to foreign merchants offer her a second source of income. Canaanite and Phoenician traders come by caravan and ship to choose out the best, the most exquisite, the most extraordinary goods to carry to distant places, and her sashes certainly qualified. Ever the business-woman, she trades, exchanges, barters, and sells her sashes and linen garments (verse 24).

A Personal Story

For me, this verse has been a special challenge. The thought of "something personal" becoming "something pro-fessional" has sparked my thoughts and fueled my energy for a long time. Just like God's beautiful woman, my "thing" just happened: It grew out of something I did every day without ever thinking much about it. You see, my "thing," my something personal, was studying the Bible. Becoming a Christian at age 28, already married for eight years and the mother of two preschoolers, I fell in love with my Bible. Through it God gave me answers to many questions and direction for my confused life. Whenever I wasn't sure about something (how to discipline my children, how to be a better wife, how to run my home, how to manage my time), God's Word always had the answer. So I made sure I spent some time each day studying my Bible.

Well, "some time each day" adds up over the decades. In the still quiet times around our house (usually *very* early in the morning or at night after Katherine and Courtney were asleep), I studied, I read, I memorized, I outlined, and I broke down God's Word into paragraphs and topics and passages. One day, when I was asked to teach a Bible study, I realized I already had the makings of about ten Bible study workbooks to choose from, all originating in my daily quiet time. As I began teaching, using my handmade-at-home-early-in-the-morning materials, women from other churches wanted to use these materials for their studies, and Christian Development Ministries was born. Soon tape albums accompanied the workbooks, and now many of those studies have become books like this one, thanks to Harvest House Publishers.[2]

Earlier, I encouraged you to find a Proverbs 31 Project—something that you do well and love to do that can bring in a little something financially for the family. Developing Bible studies and writing books has become my Proverbs 31 Project. I want to invite you to find a project, too. Look again in chapter 11 for examples of real-life women who have found their "thing." And don't forget two of God's guidelines, drawn from Proverbs 31:

• *Your family is first.* Be careful not to neglect your family to pursue your own interests. With God's help and good time management, you can take care of your family and work on your Proverbs 31 Project. Everyone is cared for *and* everyone benefits when your "something personal" (your diligent activity, willing work, attention to family finances, and wise management of the people and place of home) leads naturally—and with God's blessing—to your "something professional."

• *Give it time.* As I've said, a little time each day adds up over a lifetime. Doing something to advance your "something personal" each day ultimately adds up to something very special from which "something professional" can be born! One of my favorite quotes promises that "fifteen minutes a day devoted to one definite study will make one a master in a dozen years."[3]

The How-To's of Beauty

Once you've identified what your "thing" is—your "something personal," the area where you excel and express yourself—you'll want to actively and consciously cultivate a higher level of creativity. Here are some criteria for creativity that I try to work on every day.

1. Alertness—To nurture your creativity and stay excited about your project, make it a practice to notice how other people express themselves. Keep up with what's happening in your field. Try to stay on the cutting edge of your "thing." Stay alert and aware of other people's creative efforts. For instance, my friend Judy is an artist who stays motivated and stimulated by going to the Los Angeles County Art Museum the first Tuesday of every month (which is the "free" day). Another friend is an interior decorator who spends time walking through the fully furnished model homes in Southern California. Still another friend is a designer who wouldn't miss the latest issue of *Architectural Digest* magazine. Another artist friend has a weekly appointment for teatime with herself to linger over and study her latest issue of *Victoria* magazine. You'll continue to grow creatively if you stay alert and aware of the expressions of creativity all around you.

2. Planning—Of course you'll want to set aside time for planning your projects and developing your skills and abilities. But I also want to encourage you to use every spare minute you can find to plan and create in your mind. For instance, when Jim sold my car recently, we realized that, in the four years I had it, I never set the automatic station stops on my car radio because I've designated my car time for thinking. I carry a small dictating machine with me and speak right into that important tool my thoughts, plans, and dreams as well as any reminders to myself. The next time you're in the shower or alone in your car, use the time to plan rather than to zone out or fire up the radio. While you're waiting at the doctor's office, plan! While you're in the checkout line at the grocery store, plan! Keep your mind thinking about how to do what you do better.

3. Initiative—It takes initiative to make the phone call to enroll in a class that will help you develop your skills. It takes initiative to go to a specialty store and purchase a magazine that targets your area of creativity. It takes initiative to subscribe to a journal, magazine, newspaper, or educational cable station that will help you in your creative pursuits. It takes initiative to bring your dreams down to earth and finally set up a work station, the sewing machine, or the easel. It takes initiative to find out where to send your sample line of greeting cards, your manuscript, your book ideas, or your magazine article. It takes initiative to plan a weekend at a conference that addresses your area of interest and desired expertise.

And taking initiative—this crucial step toward a more creative lifestyle—is difficult for many women. As one of God's beautiful women, you need to not only know what you want to do in order to benefit your family, but you also have to act on that desire. Every morning, write down one thing you can do that day to turn your "something personal" into "something professional." That step may be only making a phone call or buying a helpful resource. Or it may be spending 15 minutes doing what you love. But keep in mind that 15 minutes a day will make you a master in a dozen years!

4. *Hard work*—Hard work is essential for success in any venture, and that's exactly what God's beautiful woman does: "She willingly works" (Proverbs 31:13). Besides running the home and getting meals on the table, this dear woman weaves (verses 13,19,21,24), and she excels at it to the stature of professionalism (verses 18,24). Through this Proverbs 31 Project, she provides clothes and extra income for the family. She worked hard to get her enterprise going, and she continues to work hard.

Maybe this is a good place to tell you another reason Proverbs 31:24 is such an exciting verse for me. First let me acknowledge that you may be feeling overwhelmed by the productivity of the Proverbs 31 woman. After all, she has her husband, her children, and her servants to take care of, and her food, her marketing, her fields, the production of the family's clothing, and even the poor in the community to tend to—and we haven't even gotten to the housework yet (verse 27)! The list goes on and on!

But, for me, the crowning achievement of this godly and beautiful woman is her little enterprise. By putting in the time required at home to fulfill God's high calling for her as a wife, mother, and homemaker, she improved her weaving skills and perfected her time management skills . . . until she excelled in her creative efforts. Then, when she realized that her merchandise was good, she worked even harder to get the work at home done faster so she could follow her dreams and have more time to be creative. Her hard work buys her the time she wants and needs to pursue her talent, to excel in her field, and to run her cottage industry. She is truly worthy of her well-deserved, hard-earned praise (verse 31)!

An Invitation to Beauty

I certainly hope and pray you are encouraged by the industry (pun intended!) of this magnificent woman who is beautiful in God's eyes! Our society focuses so much on self-fulfillment, self-image, and self-esteem. But the good news in Proverbs 31 is that *God* provides all that you need in these areas. After all, there is no greater fulfillment than knowing that you have loved and cared for your family and home. When you (and I) take care of your "something personal" first—the people at home—and do it well, God can grow you personally and even propel you into "something professional," something creative, some avenue where you can express the creative gifts and talents He has given you. If you have no idea where to begin your pursuit of your "something professional," start right this minute asking God to reveal what He would have you do. Just one hint. Your cottage industry will probably grow out of something you are already doing . . . or dreaming of doing!

-18-

A Wardrobe of Virtues
HER CLOTHING

෨

"Strength and dignity are her clothing;
she shall rejoice in time to come."[1]
Proverbs 31:25

I don't know you as well as I would like, but I do
know a few things about you. First of all, I can be
sure you are a woman who desires God's beauty
in her life or you wouldn't be reading a book with the title
Beautiful in God's Eyes. That's a given.

And I'm also sure about some other details of your
everyday life. You get up (and together we're working on
doing that a little earlier!), you (I hope) join with the
psalmist in saying, "This is the day which the Lord has made;
we will rejoice and be glad in it" (Psalm 118:24), and then,
at some later time in your morning, you get dressed. (How am
I doing?) Opening your closet door, you take a look.
Thinking through the events scheduled for your fresh new
day, you finally select the clothes suitable for your activities
and put them on.

Well, dear one, that's exactly how God's beautiful woman
greets the days of her life. She, too, rises up to praise the God
she loves so much, and she, too, considers the activities of
her day and then selects the appropriate garments to wear.
She doesn't have a lot of clothing to choose from (in fact, the

heavy woolen cloak people wore in her day served as their blanket at night), but she has what's adequate and proper.

The Clothing of Character

But the woman who is beautiful in God's eyes adorns herself daily with clothing that doesn't hang in her closet. Proverbs 31:25 says, "*Strength* and *dignity* are her clothing." These two prized ornaments are the most impressive part of our virtuous woman's attire because they are the clothing of godly character.

Once again we see that *strength* is an attribute of God's beautiful woman—and that strength manifests itself in a variety of ways. The Proverbs 31 woman has, for instance, faithfully built up economic strength, so she faces daily life and the prospect of old age with ample monetary reserves. Also, having made diligent preparations, she is ready to meet temporal changes (like a snowy change in the weather [verse 21]) with confidence. Her great trust in the Lord (verse 30) strengthens her for sorrow and care. Although, being a woman, she is considered "the weaker vessel" (1 Peter 3:7), she is strong in wisdom (verse 26) and in the knowledge of God (verse 30). Besides developing physical strength through the demands of her day-to-day work, she has gained social strength by her upright heart, her virtues, and her dignified conduct (verse 25). As the finishing touch to this wardrobe of virtues, her powerful mind gives her an inward vigor and resolution. Yes, strength for life is her clothing.

Dignity is another ornament this woman, who is beautiful in God's eyes, wears consistently. The literal Hebrew translation is "splendor."[2] Apparently her noble spirit gives her the aura of majesty. We marvel at her virtuous character, her regal bearing, and her godly behavior. There is nothing common, low, or little in her wardrobe of character. Her greatness of soul—coupled with her gracious conduct—spells goodness to all who are blessed to know her. All that she is, is touched with the beauty of dignity.

Joy for a Lifetime

Clothed in her rich wardrobe of virtues, God's beautiful woman "shall rejoice in time to come" (verse 25). Not only does she live in the present with utmost joy, but, in the words of another translator, "she *smiles* at the future."[3] When she looks forward—whether to a new day or to her death—"she laughs at the time to come."[4] As author Anne Ortlund shares, this woman's ability to smile and laugh at her future "puts the lines on her face in the right places"![5] Having made all human provision possible and knowing that God will take care of the rest, God's beautiful woman faces the future with joy for a lifetime. Faithful herself with the temporal matters of life, she trusts God for the eternal.

As we've noted, the Proverbs 31 woman wears only a few jewels. She wears none of the usual cheap trinkets— the anxieties, the worries, the fears—which detract from the appearance of so many others. Instead, her beauty is unmarred by concern for life's uncertainties. Whether she's thinking about the past, the present, or the future, she experiences only pleasure. She's done her job. She's carried out her God-given assignments and lived out her virtues a day at a time, every day of her life. Looking backward, she has no regrets. Looking forward, she has nothing to dread. Living in the present, she knows only the joyous challenge of tapping into God's provision and putting her powerful mind and body to work for one more beautiful and joy-filled day!

The How-To's of Beauty

These days, books, conferences, and counselors all offer to help me learn about "God's will" for my life. My choice for instruction is Proverbs 31! I love to study this passage about God's beautiful woman because it gives me—and you—concrete guidance. Every single day of our life we can know exactly what God's will for us is by reading Proverbs 31:10-31. Married or single, young or old, stay-at-home mom or working woman, we are to be about the business of becoming beautiful in God's eyes. The same virtuous traits which the young prince's mother spells out for him to seek in a wife are the traits which we are to pursue. If we do, we too will be clothed with God's strength and dignity and able to smile at the future.

As you know by now, I'm a strong believer in the value of goals. (Sometimes I even drive myself crazy! I have lifetime, ten-year, five-year, one-year, half-year, monthly, weekly, and daily goals written down, and the daily goals often are specific to the hour. In fact my timer is ticking right this second—sounding out for me a 30-minute goal!) I find it easier to set goals for daily life if I break the complexities of life into seven categories.[6] As we look at the how-to's of clothing all of life in God's garments of virtue, consider the following seven areas of godly living. And remember that right now—today!—is the day that counts. It's the only day we have. When you and I take life one day at a time, when we wake up every day for the rest of our life and dress for success in God's wardrobe of virtues, we will find ourselves clothed by God with virtues that will supply us with a life-long harvest of joy.

1. Your spiritual life—We've been talking about our clothes closet, but first let's consider your prayer closet, that place where you nurture your love for the Lord (Proverbs 31:30).

That's the closet you want to visit first each day. God called to His holy city, "Awake, awake; put on your strength, O Zion; put on your beautiful garments" (Isaiah 52:1)! He calls you and me to do the same, and the most beautiful garment in your wardrobe of virtues is your love for Him. As young Lemuel's mother stresses, "A woman who fears the Lord, she shall be praised" (verse 30). *She* is the one who is truly beautiful in God's eyes!

When you emerge from the sacred communion of your prayer closet, you'll be wearing the clothing of righteousness. You will have exchanged your spirit of heaviness for God's festive garment of praise (Isaiah 61:3). You'll also be ready for battle, having donned the whole armor of God (Ephesians 6:12-18). And no one will fail to notice the fragrance of Christ and the aroma of life in Him (2 Corinthians 2:14-16) that flows from your soul.

Why not set yourself the goal of seeking the Lord early (Psalm 63:1)? If you haven't already done so today, stop right now, put this book down, and spend time with the only Person who can make you genuinely beautiful—God Himself! You can smile at the future when you receive God's "strength for today and bright hope for tomorrow"[7] each day of your life.

2. Your family life—Whatever your circumstances, you have a family. You have parents, sisters, brothers, grandparents, aunts, uncles, nieces, nephews, or cousins to love. If you're married, you have a husband and in-laws and maybe some children to love, and you are to be pouring your life into them just as God's beautiful woman does. We all have the family of God, the body of Christ, the church.

If you want to reap the kind of rewards God's beautiful woman reaps (verses 28-29), put your family first—and be sure they know that's where they stand! Take care of their physical needs of food (verses 14-15) and clothing (verse 21). See that you run a neat, clean, orderly home (verse 27). Pour out your love—lavishly, unselfishly, creatively, and joyously. And, if your service, your care, and your love seem to be unnoticed, or you feel unappreciated, or you never hear a "thank you," keep in mind the perspective and call of Colossians 3:23— "Whatever you do, do it heartily *as to the Lord* and not unto men."

That beautiful, godly principle doesn't always earn us rave reviews, though. Just this week a friend called, sounding a little downhearted. As we talked, she shared that her sister had pointed out that she was "too nice" to her children—fixing sack lunches and leaving food in the oven for late-arriving, working adult children. I wish you could have heard the sermon I preached from Proverbs 31! God's beautiful woman takes care of her family—whatever age and whatever stage! A part of her permanent clothing is the apron of "too nice": "The fruit of the Spirit is . . . kindness [and] goodness" (Galatians 5:22-23)!

3. Your financial life—God's beautiful woman can smile when she looks to the future because she has kept watch over the household finances. She has set goals and reached them. What financial goals do you have for your day, the week, this month, and the year?

One day during the writing of this book, I got a glimpse of my daughters' goals when I received e-mail messages from both of them. Katherine was asking for all my recipes from those days when times were hard, and Courtney was telling me that she had started shopping for groceries only once every two weeks—which challenged her creativity toward the end of the second week! With these two real-life, practical, and simple methods, you can save money, too.

You can also save on clothing by waiting for sales, saying "no," and shopping only one day a week. (You burn out really fast when you have to get everything done on the same day! Believe me, you'll want to rush home and never go "out there" again!) As I shared earlier, you can also save finance fees by staying on top of the bill-paying (see chapter 4). You can open up an automatic savings account. You can ask your husband for an allowance—and save it!

The next time you're in the car or shower, think about what you might do to bring in some income. I have a girl-friend who assembles furniture for an office furniture store. She works on the family room floor after her kids are in bed. My Lori and her daughter Bethany helped me out by making my bulk mailings and workbook assembling their Proverbs 31 Projects. Another woman I know (a senior citizen) sticks labels onto cassette tapes while caring for her 100-year-old mother! With a dollars-and-cents mindset and a willingness to do the work, you can make a significant financial contribution to your future—and your present!

4. *Your physical life*—(Oh, no! We knew this would come up sooner or later!) Proverbs 31:25 speaks of the strength of God's beautiful woman. While strength is a garment in her wardrobe of virtues, it is also a part of her physical makeup. She did, after all, strengthen her body and arms *for* her work and *by* her work (verse 17).

In order to follow in her steps, I want you to set a few goals for your physical health and strength. Would you feel better if you trimmed down a little—or do you need to beef up? Strong muscle tone means fewer back, shoulder, and neck strains. (This one's a must for me! One box of my books weighs 32 pounds, and I have to lift them seven days a week and carry them up and down stairs and in and out of airports!) Exercise means fewer worries about arthritis, osteoporosis, and clogged arteries. Proper food fuels your work and betters your all-around health. You'll feel better today—and in the future you'll be smiling, too—if you tend to this vital aspect of your life and make time in your schedule to get moving.

5. *Your mental life*—The Bible calls us to love God with all our mind (Luke 10:27). (I feel so strongly about this subject that I wrote an entire book on it, *Loving God with All Your Mind*.[8]) I do believe that, as Christians, we will give an account to God for the use (and misuse) of our mind. God makes us in His image with the ability to think and learn, analyze and create (Genesis 1:27; James 3:9). Indeed, we have the mind of Christ (1 Corinthians 2:16)! Not surprisingly, then, Scripture tells us again and again what to do with our mind. (So far, I've counted 31 exhortations regarding the right and wrong ways a Christian can use her mind!)

Now for a personal challenge: How do you use your mind? If I asked how you use your *minutes*, I would be asking for the same information because every minute you're awake, you're using your *mind*. Here are some ideas for how to use your mind in constructive ways.

- As a woman desiring to become more and more beautiful in God's eyes, make sure that, first and foremost, you use your mind to read God's Word, memorize it, and meditate on it.

- You can also think through the issues of Scripture—the role of women in the church, etc.

- You can think, pray, and plan—just as the Proverbs 31 woman does. (That's one of the main reasons she can smile at the future: She has thought about it, prayed about it, and planned for it!)

- You can set a goal to read a good Christian book or biography every month.
- You can read a time- or money-management book.
- Worthwhile books on marriage, mothering, and home-making are also available.

"Dear Abby" writes her thoughts: "Just for Today . . . I will improve my mind. I will not be a mental loafer. I will force myself to read something that requires effort, thought and concentration."[9] I urge you to clothe yourself with *strength of mind* and then use that strength for God's glory and the furtherance of His purposes.

6. *Your social life*—Obviously we need to set aside great amounts of time for the Lord and for our family (that's what God's beautiful woman—and this book—are all about!), but we also need to spend time with a few good friends. Proverbs tells us that, while it's difficult to be "best friends" with a lot of people, it's important to have a few. "A man who has [many] friends must himself be friendly, but there is a friend who sticks closer than a brother" (Proverbs 18:24).

Which of your friends stick closer than a brother? Does your schedule reflect time set aside for those special people? When you are together, do you make it a point to encourage each other in the Lord, in your spiritual journeys? Are your best friends on your daily prayer list?

7. *Your professional life*—After the preceding chapter, you can better understand what I mean by the phrase "professional life." It's your enterprise, your industry, your contribution, your expertise, your "something personal" that becomes "something professional" and advances your family financially. Maybe you have a job, a career, a license, a credential, or a hobby that pays. Whatever your professional life consists of, keep your skills

sharp and your knowledge up-to-date. Make sure you're always reaching for higher levels of excellence. Continue the exercises concerning creativity (stay alert; plan and dream; take initiative to develop your skills and abilities; work hard). Do whatever you have to do to stay motivated, excited, and moving forward in your unique area of expertise and skill. If God wills, you may be doing that special work for a long time! That's what this chapter is about, about securing your future as much as humanly possible. Our job is to do all we can. God's job is to take care of the rest!

You've met her before in this book, and once again Edith Schaeffer sets an example for us. She is a woman fully clothed in strength and dignity and able to smile at the future. At age 87 she was busily writing her eighteenth book. Today, she continues to wear her wardrobe of virtues, serve the Lord, love her family, take care of her physical health, and feed her mind—at age 90!

As you peer into your future, what do you pray God will enable you to be doing at age 87 or 90? "Whatever you do, do all to the glory of God" (1 Corinthians 10:31)!

An Invitation to Beauty

Being able to rejoice in the future requires clothing yourself today with the garment of strength and the ornament of dignity. So here are a few "just for today" thoughts.

Just for today . . . give your life afresh to God and proceed full-faith ahead into your beautiful day. Just for today . . . wholeheartedly pour out your love and care for your family and be "too nice"! Just for today . . . think about your positive contributions to the family finances. Just for today . . . take your physical "strength" seriously and exert yourself. Just for today . . . eliminate the misuse of your mind and instead use that brain power God has given you to grow more beautiful in character. Just for today . . . reach out and encourage your best friend in her spiritual journey. Just for today . . . take one small step toward your "something professional." Finally, just for today . . . make the commitment to wake up every day of your life and repeat this pattern for beauty. Then you, too, can stand fully robed in your virtues, look down the corridor of time toward your unknown future, and rejoice!

-19-

A Law of Kindness
HER WORDS

⌒⌒

"She opens her mouth with wisdom,
and on her tongue is the law of kindness."[1]
Proverbs 31:26

Well, how are you doing so far on our climb toward excellence? I thought we had better pause a moment and see how we're faring. We're getting ready to take a giant step, and I want to be sure you can make it! In chapter 1, you and I decided to look steadfastly at God's idea of beauty and take the necessary steps, one after the other, to reach the heights of His ideal. And we're making wonderful progress!

Just think of all we've learned—and, I hope, begun to put into practice. We've found, for instance, that getting up just a little earlier *is* possible! We see that running our life and home on a schedule is paying off! Nurturing our marriage is bringing great personal satisfaction. Energy flows as we busy ourselves in constructive activity. Finances are firming up as we diligently manage, save, and earn money. Our involvement in ministry blesses us—and others. Taking care of our family's needs brings us deep joy. And God is using our obedience to work His godly character in us. God's ways do work!

But now, dear one, as we approach another virtue of beauty—indeed a crowning glory!—we must once again count the cost of our journey. This virtue just may be the one that truly separates the women from the girls in God's army. I warn you, it's probably the hardest to achieve! I'm talking about controlling the quality of the words that come from our mouth.

Oh, we've come a long way and climbed a far piece, but this matter of the tongue trips up many women in their journey toward becoming beautiful in God's eyes. Beautiful speech is hard-won. It's a minute-by-minute challenge. As one of the apostles writes, "If anyone does not stumble in word, he is a perfect man" (James 3:2)!

I'll be frank. Being committed to our home, running the household in an organized manner, excelling in meal preparation and homemaking, supporting our husband's advancement, giving generously to charity, and bringing in income are all easy—compared to opening our mouth with wisdom and kindness. Why do I say that? Because actions are externals, but speech is a matter of the heart: "Out of the abundance of the heart [the] mouth speaks" (Luke 6:45). To be truly beautiful in God's eyes, you and I must push ahead and take this next difficult-but-beautiful step toward more godly speech. God wants His laws of wisdom and kindness to govern our speech—and our heart.

A Fountain of Life

Before we consider the words that we speak, remember that the setting of Proverbs 31 is the deadly dry land of Israel. Hardship was—and is—the rule of the day. Survival was—and is—a day-in, day-out challenge. Brutal heat and life-threatening thirst are two facts of daily life. I wish I could adequately describe for you how great and how relentlessly daily the people's concern about having adequate water is in this parched and arid land. Given your choice of food or water, you would always choose water!

Against this harsh background, the writer of Proverbs paints this image: "The mouth of the righteous is a fountain of life" (Proverbs 10:11, NASB). The writer knows how important water is in sustaining life, and he compares godly speech to life-giving water. He likens the effect of godly speech on our emotional needs to that of water on our physical needs. Just as finding a fountain in the desert was the same as finding life, being in the presence of a woman who speaks words of wisdom and kindness is like finding life!

Wise in Speech

The speech of God's beautiful woman truly is a fountain of life to those around her. Lemuel's mother continues, "She *opens* her mouth with wisdom" (Proverbs 31:26). Note an important thought right away. The wording suggests that her mouth is not always open! She's not a yapper or a compulsive talker or a jabber-mouth. Unless she has something wise and kind to say, her mouth is shut.

When she does speak, "she opens her mouth with *wisdom.*" She is wise in what she says and how she says it. Wisdom has long been defined as "the use of knowledge in a practical and successful way."[2] Simply scan through Proverbs 31 and note the practical topics young Prince Lemuel's mother covered. She herself opened her mouth to impart wisdom—practical knowledge for living—to her precious son.

Kind in Heart

As Proverbs 31:26 continues, we see that "on her tongue is the *law of kindness.*" Not only does the woman we're admiring let wisdom guide her speech, but she also limits it according to the law of kindness. All that she utters is in the *spirit* and *manner* of a gentle and benevolent heart, revealing a kindly disposition and a fear of unnecessarily offending.[3] She acquires wisdom and limits her words accordingly. She is never hurtful or destructive with her words. As the Greek translation puts it, "she places order on her tongue."[4]

Now think for a moment about the daily life of God's beautiful woman. She has her husband—whom she is intent upon encouraging and blessing. She has children—whom she must instruct, train, and discipline. Servants—who need directions for the day—reside in her home. Merchants and buyers—who must be dealt with as she barters, bargains, and buys—are on her trade route. Every person in her life means words must be spoken, and the Proverbs 31 woman makes sure her words are wise and kind.

A note of interest (and challenge!) here: In ancient Jewish marriages, not only was the content of a woman's speech important, but *the volume of her voice* was important as well. A woman could be divorced without a marriage settlement if she had a loud voice! How was "loud" measured? By the ability of her neighbors to hear her speak while in her own house.[5] Take heed!

Absence of Malice

What's true in art is also true of speech: What is *not* present makes a louder statement than what is. In light of that, consider what is absent from the words of God's beautiful woman.

For starters, there is no gossip, slander, or unkindness toward others. Kindness would never do that! Nor is there any complaining. As a woman who fears the Lord, God's beautiful woman knows that because He maintains perfect control over the circumstances of life, she really has nothing to complain about! Wit, humor, and jesting—especially at other people's expense—are not how she wants to make her mark. Our beautiful lady would rather be known for her wisdom than her ability to entertain. And, opening her mouth wisely, she certainly says nothing indiscreet or unwholesome. Meaningless talk of trivia and trifles has also been erased from her speech. As a successful estate manager and businesswoman, she could be tempted to speak with an assertive voice, but again kindness rules her rhetoric.

As one student of human nature has so aptly noted, "Those who are not gracious talk of the wrong things. Those who are gracious but not wise talk too much." Wisdom and the law of kindness prevent both errors.

Listening to God's Beautiful Women

When looking through Scripture for wise women who observe the gracious law of kindness, I found two of God's beautiful women who shine forth as models for us in this delicate and difficult area of controlling our tongue.

Hannah is a woman who opened her mouth *very little* under *very difficult* circumstances! Married to a man who had another wife, Hannah endured not only childlessness as her rival bore child after child, but also cruel and ongoing provocations from that woman (1 Samuel 1:1-7). Again and again insult was added to injury, yet Hannah chose to say nothing in response.

With great agony of soul, she went to the house of the Lord (the right place and the right Person) to pray about her situation (the right solution). The intensity of her praying caused the high priest to think she must be drunk, and he said scornfully, "How long will you be drunk? Put your wine away from you" (verse 14). But dear, noble Hannah answered with wisdom and according to the law of kindness, graciously explaining her pain and appealing to his understanding. In the end, she received his priestly blessing.

Abigail, whose name means "source of joy," is a woman who lived out the proverb "The mouth of the righteous is a fountain of life" (Proverbs 10:11, NASB). Married to the foolish, alcoholic Nabal (his name even means "foolish"), Abigail used some carefully chosen words to successfully walk a tightrope of danger. When her husband rebuffed David's kindnesses and mistreated his men (1 Samuel 25:10-11), her servants reported Nabal's insulting behavior to her. She intercepted David on his mission to annihilate all that belonged to Nabal—including herself and the servants. Acting quickly—and with wisdom and kindness—Abigail met David with abundant food for his 600 men.

Then, prostrate on the ground before the enraged David, Abigail begged his forgiveness. With her sensible reasoning and words of wisdom spoken in accordance with the law of kindness, she successfully persuaded David not to take vengeance on her husband. Returning home to find her husband too drunk to listen, she wisely said nothing of the danger that had been avoided until the next day. Abigail worked wisely to keep both David and Nabal from making rash moves. She lives on in history as a wise woman, a skillful negotiator, and a persuasive speaker.[6]

It's encouraging to know that you and I can follow in the footsteps of these two wise and beautiful women!

The How-To's of Beautiful Speech

Oh, my dear friend, I wish I had space to tell you of the years I've been struggling toward beautiful speech! I detailed at length my battle with gossip in my book *A Woman After God's Own Heart.*[7] I've been learning how and when to talk

to and about my husband and children (less is always best!).
I've stumbled through the preschool, school-age, teenage,
and young-adults-living-at-home years of raising my girls. I
can only say that I know *God knows* how desperately I was
trying—and I keep trying because this principle of wise and
kind speech is God's beautiful plan and His clear standard for
my life and my lips.

The Book of Proverbs, tucked into the middle of your
Bible, offers invaluable, eternal wisdom, including some of
God's rules for godly speech. I'm delighted to share a few of
them with you—the ones that have helped me the most and
still do!

1. *Establish two guidelines*—God's beautiful woman set
two guidelines for her speech: 1) Speak only if the words are
wise, and 2) speak only if the words are kind (Proverbs
31:26). By following these same two guidelines, you will
always have something to say that's worth saying (wisdom),
and you'll say it in the right way (with kindness)! You can
know a lot, but if you speak unkindly, your words will be less
effective.

2. *Think before you speak*—"The heart of the righteous
studies how to answer, but the mouth of the wicked pours
forth evil" (Proverbs 15:28). Literally pause and think about
your words before you speak them. Make it your goal to carefully select wording that measures up to God's standards of
wisdom and kindness. When you aren't careful, evil "gushes
like a torrent"![8] Rash speech and quick temper betray a
shallow and less than beautiful character.[9]

3. *Learn to wait*—When something unpleasant happens, make it your first "law" to do and say nothing. If you
must respond at the moment, be sure your words are soft
because "a *soft* answer turns away wrath, but a harsh word

stirs up anger" (Proverbs 15:1). Then wait. Waiting buys you time to:

- Search the Scriptures and find out what God says about how to handle the situation.
- Seek counsel and find out what other wise people say. As Proverbs 15:14 cautions, "Where there is no counsel, the people fall." Proverbs 28:26 warns, "He who trusts in his own heart is a fool."
- Pray for a kind heart and a wise solution for the situation.
- Calm down! Cool down! Back off! As Proverbs 17:27 says, "A man of understanding is of a calm spirit." Only when we are calm can we hear good counsel and make wise decisions.
- Weigh the problem. Decide whether the situation is something to pass over (Proverbs 19:11) or whether you need to "open" your mouth and address (with wisdom and kindness, of course!) the people involved.
- Consider the person involved: Is the offense out of character, or is it becoming a pattern? Is it a one-time failure or another in a string of repeated misbehavior?

4. *Add sweetness to your speech*—Wisdom possesses great charm when sweetened with the right words. That truth is behind Proverbs 16:21—"Sweetness of the lips increases learning." Speaking pleasantly will always make others more willing to listen and be instructed. It's true that a spoonful of sugar makes the medicine go down!

5. *Add persuasiveness to your speech*—Besides being kind and speaking sweetly, know what you're talking about. Your speech will always be an indicator of what is in your mind, and you want to display knowledge when you speak. When you speak with authority, when it's obvious you know what

you're talking about, your words will be persuasive. True wisdom cannot fail to make a good impression.

6. *Err on the side of less*—When it comes to words, less is always best! Proverbs 10:19 says, "In the multitude of words sin is not lacking, but he who restrains his lips is wise." Proverbs 17:28 points out that "even a fool is counted wise when he holds his peace." In contemporary language, "Better to be quiet and be thought a fool than to speak and remove all doubt!"

Clearly, when we follow God's two standards of wisdom and kindness, our speech will be beautiful. May God grow us into women of whom it can be said, "She opens her mouth with wisdom, and on her tongue is the law of kindness" (Proverbs 31:26).[10]

An Invitation to Beauty

Now, my faithful, gallant climbing companion, I want you to think again about that fountain in the desert, the one that is a fountain of life. Then think of the hurting, stressed, struggling people who fill your daily world. While they may wear brave smiles, another proverb reveals the truth behind every smile: "The heart knows its own bitterness. . . . Even in laughter the heart is sorrowful, and the end of that mirth is heaviness" (Proverbs 14:10 and 13, KJV).

Won't you join me in making a commitment to refresh and encourage, to cheer and uplift the hearts of all you encounter with life-giving words, with words that are wise and kind? You can be a fountain of life. Rather than being "one who speaks like the piercings of a sword," yours could be "the tongue of the wise [that] promotes health" (Proverbs 12:18). With God's blessing, His love in your heart, and your careful choice of wise and kind words, you can help heal the downhearted.

And when you fail, dear one, remember this alphabet of wisdom regarding beautiful speech: **A**ccept God's challenge of speaking only wise and kind words, **B**e not discouraged, and **C**ontinue to try! That's how you and I can continue to reach toward God's beautiful standard!

-20-

A Watchful Eye
HER MANAGEMENT

⌒

"She watches over the ways of her household,
and does not eat the bread of idleness."
Proverbs 31:27

So what did you do today?" I can expect this cheerful greeting from my sweet husband every single day when he arrives home from work. Glad to be home and content to make small talk, Jim graciously turns his attention my way. After a challenging day at work, he wants to know about my day. His genuine thoughtfulness always amazes me—but it also makes my heart race because for some reason my mind homes straight in on that little word *do*—"So, what did you *do* today?" Even though Jim is not asking in order to hold me accountable, I'm so tuned in to accountability myself that I automatically answer, "I don't know exactly what I did, but I do know one thing—I never sat down all day long!"

Such vigilance about how wisely and effectively I spend my time has not always been the case for me! But that was before I learned one dynamite lesson from God's beautiful woman, a lesson about time, life, and home management: The woman who is beautiful in God's eyes "watches over the ways of her household, and does not eat the bread of idleness" (Proverbs 31:27). The wisdom from this verse—showing me

201

vividly what I should do and should not do—gave me a double-barreled challenge for a lifetime. First, the positive.

Keeping Watch Over Her Flock

Teaching us even more about the woman who is beautiful in God's eyes, Prince Lemuel's mother says: "She *watches* over the ways of her household" (Proverbs 31:27). We know the Proverbs 31 woman has the finances for servants (verse 15), but here we see that she is actively involved in the hands-on management of her household. No one runs her home for her. It's *her* home, *her* family, *her* household, and she considers its management an area of *her* stewardship.

Using an image familiar to her young son (the boy who would one day be king and "watch over" his people), his mother describes his future wife as a watchman. Charged to be an observant and careful lookout, a watchman guarded and watched over a city or a field. Lemuel had grown up seeing watchmen stationed 24 hours a day on the city walls, watch towers, and hilltops. They were to be on the alert for hostile action and report any kind of suspicious activity to the king.[1] Young Lemuel knew exactly what a watchman was and what a watchman did.

His wise mother, a master manager herself, tells her son to marry the kind of woman who will "watch over" his family and household affairs, a woman with—as the expression goes—eyes in the back of her head! As the one keeping watch, the woman turns her head, looking everywhere so that she doesn't miss a single detail![2] This imagery of the watch-keeper suggests that she stands guard, moving her eyes back and forth to see who is coming and who is going, in order to fulfill her divine assignment as overseer of her precious family and property. She keeps a good watch and oversees everything.

Just how seriously does God's beautiful watch-keeper take her stewardship? The King James Version says, "She [looks] *well* to the ways of her household" (Proverbs 31:27). In other words, she doesn't just glance over things or check the temperature at home (literally and figuratively) only once in a while, but she looks closely, intently studying the situation and overseeing everything that pertains to her home. Alert and energetic, she has her finger on the pulse of her household; nothing escapes her scrutiny and control.[3] You see, her job assignment from God is to maintain a watchful eye, to know all about what's going on under her roof, and to care for the people as well as the place.

Next we see that "she watches over the *ways* of her household" (Proverbs 31:27). She carefully notices the patterns of her home life—the "ways" of her household, the general comings and goings, the habits and activities of the people at home. The Hebrew word for *ways* means literal tracks made by constant use. They're like the foot path that appears through the lawn or the road created by heavy traffic.[4] Our watch-woman is aware of these habits and any changes in habits. Nothing catches her by surprise!

God's beautiful overseer observes all that goes on in her home. She keeps up-to-the-minute on the status of her family members and the general flow of her home. She's aware of everything that goes on within its walls. Just as the watchman for the city reports any suspicious or potentially harmful actions to the king, so God's beautiful woman sounds the alarm when necessary. When a situation goes awry, she sounds the warning to her husband. She remains faithful as his watcher.

Ever faithful, "she watches over the ways of her *household*." And that household extends beyond the members of her immediate family. Her husband and her children are her greatest concern. They are her sheep; their well-being and activities are her first concern. But, in addition to these sheep and any literal flocks she may have (Proverbs 31:17 and Proverbs 27:23), our beautiful woman also has the flock of her household. As the mistress of her household, she also cares for any extended family members and her servants, watching over them, too, as a shepherd watches over his flock.

Keeping Watch Over Herself

The woman who is beautiful in God's eyes watches over herself as well: "She does not eat the bread of idleness" (Proverbs 31:27). The Hebrew for *eating* suggests a lifestyle of "good living," but God's beautiful woman is *not* engaging in "the good life"! On the contrary, she chooses not to live a leisurely life filled with food and drink.[5] She who vigilantly watches over her household has no place for idleness in her schedule. How could she afford to be idle? How could she even find the time? Busy managing her house and watching over her flock, she has no time to partake of ("eat of") laziness and idleness. This truth could also be flipped: Because she is not idle, she has the time she needs to keep a watchful eye on her home and be sure that it's well-managed!

In Proverbs 31:27 ("She does not eat the bread of idleness"), it's also interesting to note that the Hebrew for "bread" is a word associated with sluggishness. The use of "bread" together with "eat" paints a clear picture: God's beautiful woman has no part in sluggishness of any kind. One translation tells us she is "not content to go through life eating and sleeping."[6] My favorite commentary simply states, "She is never lazy"![7] Now do you understand why I never sit down? Proverbs 31:27 challenges me for a lifetime!

The How-To's of Beauty

First the people—A good principle to remember when it comes to life under your roof is, "The people first, then the place." The precious people who make up your family will always be far more important than the place where you live. After all, the place exists to serve the people. So your beautiful role is to see that the people at home are cared for spiritually, emotionally, and physically. Your job assignment from God requires you to make sure your family members have food and clothing—just as the Proverbs 31 woman did!

In light of that charge, read these haunting words written by wife, mother, grandmother, and great-grandmother Edith Schaeffer: "Neglected mothers and grandmothers may perhaps have been preparing for their own neglect by teaching over and over again that people's sensitive feelings, and people's need of response is never as important as clean houses, schedules, or rules and regulations."[8] When you follow the precept "the people first, then the place," you'll always be focusing your energy in the right place—the place for maximum beauty.

Part of caring for the people is praying for them. As the psalmist says, "Unless the Lord builds the house, they labor in vain who build it; unless the Lord guards the city [or house], the watchman stays awake in vain" (Psalm 127:1). On this side of heaven, you will never know how many discouraged family members have been encouraged by your prayers for them, how many problems have been solved because God granted wisdom given in response to your requests, or how many spiritual battles were won under your roof because you lifted your entreaties beyond your roof to the throne of heaven!

Then the place—With the people at home cared for, you can turn your attention to your "household management." I have on my desk a massive old volume from 1861 entitled

Beeton's Book of Household Management[9] given to me by a friend living in Scotland. Its 1125 pages detail information on the raising, selecting, killing, dressing, butchering, preserving, and preparing of animals for consumption, how to serve a meal for nineteen, the duties and proper manner of instruction for cooks, maids, coachmen, laundry maids, nurses, etc., who will carry out some of those tasks, and medical and legal information. This manual was definitely intended to assist any woman who desired to watch over and look well to the ways of her household!

I was thinking about what we who are God's beautiful women do to watch over our homes, and I want to share my list which—like yours—is different from Beeton's! Like the Proverbs 31 woman, though, I watch over my house—over the people, the place, the finances, the meals, the "maids," and the clothes. For instance, right now my washing machine (my laundry maid) is spinning away. I've already turned on the sprinklers (my gardener), closed up and cooled down the house (it's August!), delivered a car to be worked on (my coachman assisted), and enjoyed breakfast with my husband (a meal and time of companionship). I've e-mailed both my daughters, still "watching over" them and nurturing relationships from long distance. The house is tidied, the bills are paid, the mail is out in the mailbox, phone calls have been returned, and the day's work is planned. I met with the Lord and He encouraged my heart and strengthened me to handle another fast-paced, demanding day. It's 11:30 A.M. now, and I've been seeking from my first waking moment today to set my home and family on the right path, the right "way."

When Katherine and Courtney were younger, each day followed the same path except there was also homework for me to watch over and their chores to check up on. I invested time and effort in training Katherine and Courtney so they would one day have the skills they would need to watch over their own homes—skills like housecleaning, cooking, setting the table, taking care of the dog, maintaining the yard, and washing, folding, and ironing clothes. I ingrained certain disciplines like cleanliness, ritualistic toothbrushings, and getting to school on time—and with a sack lunch!

Having already spent six or seven hours watching over my home, now I'll begin my job of writing, with breaks for another meal with Jim tonight, another errand to pick up his car at the end of the day, the final cleanup, and probably another couple of hours of writing before bedtime. But at least I don't have to wring a chicken's neck!

Please pardon me for taking the time and space to list the activities of my days. But I want you to realize—whether you have a job or not—that looking well to the ways of your household and keeping a watchful eye involves many, many things. Any job responsibilities and loyalties at work come after the top priorities of family and home have been fulfilled. I don't write (and I research and write about ten hours a day) until I've looked after the people and the place. For me that takes about eight hours a day! My "job" of writing and teaching can never be a reason to neglect watching over the ways of my household!

And the same is true for you, too. The income from a job can never substitute for your careful watch over family and home. The woman who is beautiful in God's eyes (not necessarily in the eyes of an employer, a supervisor, a boss, the women in the office, or [gulp!] a publisher) makes sure her management at home is beautifully attended to. The joke that reports, "Most homes nowadays seem to be on three shifts—Father is on the night shift, Mother is on the day shift, and the children shift for themselves" must never be true in the beautiful home you are building for God! With a heart set on God's kind of beauty, some good time-management skills, and a plan for your day, you can manage all that life brings your way.

An Invitation to Beauty

I know it may not seem very inviting or sound very exciting, but your home is definitely the place most worthy of your diligent watching. In fact, home is the most important place in the world for you to be spending your time and investing your energy. Why do I say that? Because the work you do in "a little place" like home is eternal work, meaningful work, important work—when you realize that the work you do in your home is your supreme service to God! I invite you to enjoy the beauty of serving in a little place, a little place . . . like home.

A Little Place

"Where shall I work today, dear Lord?"
And my love flowed warm and free.
He answered and said,
"See that little place?
Tend that place for Me."

I answered and said, "Oh no, not there!
No one would ever see.
No matter how well my work was done,
Not that place for me!"

His voice, when He spoke, was soft and kind,
He answered me tenderly,
"Little one, search that heart of thine,
Are you working for them or ME?
Nazareth was a little place . . .
so was Galilee."[10]

-21-

A Cup of Blessing
HER FAMILY

_cᏳ_

"Her children rise up and call her blessed,
and her husband also, and he praises her."
Proverbs 31:28

As I write this chapter Jim and I are preparing for a trip. We're going to a surprise party for a wonderful couple in their seventies. The party is being given by their sons and daughters. It's not their fiftieth wedding anniversary, it's not a retirement party, and it's not a birthday party either. The invitation simply declares the event to be "a celebration of honor." Isn't that a wonderful idea?

Well, my beautiful friend, this chapter is also a celebration of honor. For twenty chapters you and I have listened in on a mother describing for her son a woman who is beautiful in God's eyes. Together we've drunk in her noble qualities—her diligence, her hard work, her early rising, her careful preparations, her wise management, her enterprising spirit, her encouraging speech, her attentive watch over her loved ones, and her drive to excel for the good of her family. Motivated by love, God's beautiful woman delights in pouring out her life for her family. Hers is a rare kind of beauty indeed (verse 10)!

And now we hear of a celebration in her honor. God's beautiful woman is receiving her highest reward—not from the community or the townspeople or folks at church, at work, or in the neighborhood. Her cup of blessing comes from those who matter most, those who know her best, and those who have received a lifetime of the first fruits of her day-in, day-out love—her family! Let's listen in as her children praise her.

A Blessed Mother

Proverbs 31:28 proclaims, "Her children rise up and call her blessed." We've not seen them or met them, but here, in unison, the offspring of God's beautiful woman "rise up" and sing her praises! I had to chuckle at one interpretation I read: "They rise up in the morning and, finding everything well prepared, the children express their thankfulness to her."[1] Such a display of gratitude is certainly what all moms dream of and train their children toward, but such thankfulness isn't always expressed. Another commentator suggested that rising up means standing up in her presence as a mark of respect (another one of a mother's fantasies!).[2] Still another possibility is that the children rise up as a preparatory movement in order to make an announcement, to give words of tribute in reverential honor of her,[3] much like getting up to make a speech at a special ceremony.

These interpretations may work for you, but more realistically the words *rise up* mean that the Proverbs 31 woman's children grow up and go out to live in a way that brings honor and blessing and credit to her. The children's lives become the living praise of her worth and her work.

My blessed friend, whichever meaning is intended, one thing is clear: The children of our Proverbs 31 woman give her life its highest reward. They bless her. They praise her. The children experience the sweet fruits of her virtues, and she experiences the sweet fruits of their lives and rejoices in them. As I said, they bless her—and she is blessed (which means happy)![4] Their sincere words as well as their very lives bless her. Truly her cup of blessing overflows!

Praying that my children would also "rise up"—not to say "thank you," or stand when I enter a room, or even give a speech, but that they live godly lives—caused me to examine my heart and soul. Those times of prayer also helped me identify some essential elements in the love of a mother who is a blessing to her family. These basics are a matter of the heart—the heart of a mother, *your* heart—and apply to love for children, stepchildren, and grandchildren.

Essential #1: A Mother Cares

A mother shares her love daily with her children through *the gift of the basics*—food, clothing, shelter, and rest. A popular kitchen plaque reads, "Divine services rendered here three times a day!" That's a wonderful perspective on the care we mothers offer our children as we follow in the path of the Proverbs 31 mother: She looks well to her children's ways, spending the majority of each day providing food and clothing for her loved ones. The shelter she offers includes a home warm not only in temperature but in love. Because it goes against her character to be contentious (Proverbs 21:9) or loud (Proverbs 7:11), her home is a shelter where her family can rest and know peace. Daily she extends the cup of physical care for her family.

Motherly care also means pouring out *the gift of time*. Every minute—indeed every second—we spend with our children matters! Love is spelled T-I-M-E—time, time, and more time; time in terms of minutes and time in terms of years. Indeed, our children call for a lifetime of time! Our very young children need our time—and lots of it! Did you know that 50 percent of a child's character and personality development takes place by age three and 75 percent by age five? Our children need our time when they're older, too. As they learn to reason and become real conversationalists, as they face the challenges of junior high and high school, as they become young adults in the workplace or in college, they need the gift of time from us. And they need our time when they're even older, when they are ready to be our friends. The children of the Proverbs 31 woman—who have become her *friends*—rise up to bless her! Every minute—indeed every second—we spend giving the gift of time to our children is an investment in their character and in their future.

A mother's care doesn't cease when the children are no longer at home. Instead a mother goes to work giving *the gift of long-distance love*. The beautiful Old Testament mother Hannah lavished long-distance love on her little Samuel (1 Samuel 2:19). Despite a distance of a day's journey, Samuel knew he was loved because Hannah (also a weaver) spent every year making him a new coat, which she delivered to him in person at the annual feast in the house of the Lord.

Author Elisabeth Elliot rises up and blesses her mother for letters written and sent over long distances. She exclaims, "How rich we were not to have been able to afford long-distance phone calls! Few families today have the permanent and intimately detailed record which now lies in a box in my attic—the complete set of Mother's letters to her children from 1954 through 1985."[5] When Mrs. Elliot first went away to school, her mother wrote to her twice a week. There was never a week in her life from September 1941 through the mid-1980s when she began to fail mentally that Katharine Howard did not write to her children—all six of them! This mother's letters were the overflow of a mother-heart filled with love, and that love found a way to care across long distances. This outpouring of care took time. Imagine writing a dozen letters a week—and without a word processor! Living out her love, a mother takes care of her children and gives the gift of time.

Essential #2: A Mother Focuses

As God's beautiful mothers, you and I gladly focus all our mothering energies and efforts on one goal: to raise each child to love our Lord. Our assignment from God is to raise a man or a woman who will serve and honor Him. Our focus is not on raising a doctor, a teacher, an engineer, an athlete, or even a minister or a missionary. We'll allow God to decide our child's vocation while we focus instead on raising an individual who has a heart after God. Moses was a shepherd, but his heart belonged to God. David, too, was a shepherd, Paul a tentmaker, and Peter a fisherman, but each had a heart dedicated to God.

What a privilege to join together with God and train up the next generation, the people who will, in turn, train up the generation that comes after them (Proverbs 22:6)! Mother, grandmother, and great-grandmother Edith Schaeffer explains: "We are responsible for 'handing on the flag [of faith]' and for being very careful not to drop it—or to drop out—because of our responsibility to the next generation. . . . To hand down truth to one more generation is one of the central commands of God."[6]

As you work to pass on your faith, I encourage you to pray over your children each night. Consider, for example, the heart-cry of the mother of Dr. Harry Ironside, who was known in the late nineteenth century as the "Boy Preacher of Los Angeles" and who later was pastor of Moody Memorial Church in Chicago and the author of more than 60 books. Each night his mother Sophia poured out this prayer over her son as she tucked him into bed: "Father, save my boy early. Keep him from ever desiring anything else than to live for Thee. . . . O Father, make him willing to be kicked and cuffed, to suffer shame or anything else for Jesus' sake."[7] Mrs. Ironside focused on one thing and one thing only for her child—that he would love God!

Essential #3: A Mother Plans

The beautiful mother of Proverbs 31 planned for progress in her roles (verses 15, 27), and you and I need to plan, too. Final outcomes are always in God's hands, but the daily oper-ation of the home is in ours. So let me share with you what I want (and wanted) for my family and how I plan (and planned) for it. Things as grand as these desires of my heart (and I'm sure of your heart, too) simply won't happen without planning for them!

First and foremost, I want the dynamic *presence of the Lord* in my home. This means filling my heart first. It means scheduling some prime time for God's Word and for prayer so that I bear the mark of a woman who is beautiful in God's eyes. For God's presence to be obvious in my home, my homemaking, and my dealings with the family, He must be present in my own heart.

The next thing I wanted as a young mom was to *pass on faith in Jesus Christ* to my children (grandchildren count here, too). Once again, planning helped. I planned for regular church attendance as well as for daily devotions with my girls. I even, in prayer, planned to speak of the Lord to them and asked God to help me be aware of opportunities to point my daughters to Him. My plans included surrounding Katherine and Courtney with people who shared my faith. Believe it or not, I also had to plan to pray so that I could pray for *them* regularly! I planned bedtime rituals and found Bible books and Bible stories to read to my children. Passing on your faith in Christ to your children is certainly worth some planning.

A pleasant atmosphere in the home creates a beautiful background for happy memories. Because I want the warm atmosphere and the good memories it fosters, I plan for it. I plan the meals, including how I'll set the dinner table and make it beautiful. I plan for order in the home, for the housework, for the laundry, and for the upkeep of our clothing so that life is calmer. I plan surprises, too, so that life at home is fun. If all this planning sounds like a lot of effort, remember that no work of art is slapdashed together. Artistry calls for planning and design, and so does the work of art called "Home."

I want *progressing relationships* with my children, so I plan for that. My plans include what words to speak, what questions to ask, what ways to express my love, and what special gifts and deeds of kindness to extend to them. I plan outings, holidays, and Christmas, Easter, and birthday celebrations.

Another kind of planning for relationships is planning for the bits and blocks of time you know you'll have. For instance, when your child runs in one door after school to change clothes and rushes out the other door to get to work or ball practice, when you only have a few minutes, plan for those crucial minutes. When you have only a few hours with your children—the day's been hectic, but you do have mealtime before they go out again—plan for those precious hours (and the meal, too)! Or when you only have your children, stepchildren, or grandchildren for a few days, plan to fill those days with love. You can fill every minute, hour, and day with blessings for your children!

My Katherine and Courtney are married now, but I continue to nurture my relationships with them and their husbands, so (you guessed it!) I plan for it! Writing and e-mailing my daughters, praying for them and their families, giving little gifts that help them in their married lives, helping in the ways needed, visiting them, loving their children, and celebrating holidays—I plan for all these things. And sometimes I even plan not to call or bother them!

The development of one final plan is imperative: You must plan for *persistence;* you must plan to keep on mothering—no matter what! I heard a life-changing (actually a mother-changing!) radio interview with Dr. Richard Mayhue, Dean of The Master's Seminary and a father of grown children. Dr. Mayhue likened parenting to a 100-yard football field that has a life-and-death game being played on it. He pointed out that some parents drive up to the junior high school curb (the 50-yard line), open the car door, drop the kids off, wave good-bye, and say, "Well, we've taught you everything you need to know. Now go and do it!" Then there is the parent who hands the teenager the car keys (and sometimes a car) at age sixteen (the 75-yard line), stands in the driveway, waves good-bye, and yells, "Well, you're on your own now. You can drive, you're old enough to get a job, and you know what you ought to do. Good luck!" Most parents, however, drop their still-moldable child off after high-school graduation (the 95-yard line) and call out to them, "Don't forget to visit us once in a while!"

What Dr. Mayhue stressed was "going the distance" with your child, especially between the 95-yard line and the goal at the 100-yard line, those ages of 18 to 25-ish. He described the brutal blows, the scratching, and the clawing that happen in a real football game as a team struggles to gain every inch of those final five yards. As he wisely pointed out, the final five yards is where your child chooses a career and a mate—the two most important decisions (next to faith in Jesus Christ) they make in their lives!

All of this to say, dear friend and devoted mother, you and I must plan to encourage, assist, advise, and pray for our children, whatever their ages. Our assignment calls for us to lock arms together with them and move forward shoulder to shoulder, inch by inch, all the way to the finish line—no matter what! Our care and guidance can never cease. And, trust me, your children will rise up and bless you for your persistent and prayerful mothering!

Since space is limited, I'm unable to share with you the many other deep convictions I have about what God's Word teaches us about mothering and the many lessons I've learned raising my own children, but I gladly recommend the four chapters in my book *A Woman After God's Own Heart*[8] about "The Heart of a Mother." After all, mothering truly is a matter of the heart—*your* heart!

Essential #4: A Mother Works

Instead of a section on "The How-To's of Beauty," I want to share one more essential that certainly covers some how-to's of mothering: A mother follows God's plan as she does the work of raising her children. You see, love has work to do—hard and self-sacrificing work. In the 19 verses about the Proverbs 31 woman we've looked at so far, I've counted twelve to fifteen obvious and veiled references to her work. We know that she rises while it is still dark and that her lamp does not go out when night falls (verses 15,18). From early in the morning until late at night, she's busy working for her family and doing so because of her great love for them.

Once again hear the heartfelt words of Edith Schaeffer: "Being a mother is worth fighting for, worth calling a career, worth the dignity of hard work."[9] And believe me, being a mother is the hardest work we will ever do! A mother's love is to-the-end, all-the-way work! But consider what your work as a mother can accomplish:

- A mother loves her children.

    Work puts your love into action.
- A mother cares for her children.

    Work gives your loving care expression.
- A mother focuses on making Christ known to her children.

    Work (and especially God's work in their hearts) puts feet on your faith.

As you and I do the hard work of mothering, God blesses our efforts and helps us realize our dreams for our family.

A word now about how we are to do this work. God's Word tells us that we are to work without murmuring or complaining (Philippians 2:14). God's word tells us that we are to work as unto the Lord and not unto men (Colossians 3:23). We are to work willingly and joyfully (Proverbs 31:13). We are to work expecting nothing in return (Luke 6:35). And we are to work—teaching, training, disciplining, caring, planning, giving, praying, and believing—because doing so is a mother's assignment from God!

But What If . . . ?

I can almost hear you thinking, "But what if my children don't follow my spiritual and practical leading? What if they don't live for God? What if they don't follow in the way I've trained them? What if they never say thank you or even seem to notice all I've done for them? What if they don't ever rise up in any kind of honor?"

I've had all these thoughts myself, but I've learned that a mother's energy and efforts must never be motivated by possible rewards. You see, God has determined your role: as a mother, you are to love your children—no matter what (Titus 2:4); you are to teach your children—no matter what (Proverbs 1:8); you are to train your children—no matter what (Proverbs 22:6); you are to discipline your children—no matter what (Proverbs 29:17); and you are to care for your children—no matter what (Proverbs 31:27).

Even when a mother wonders if her efforts will result in the godly children she prays for, she keeps on doing these things. Why? Because in her heart she has faith not in her doing, but in God! So a mother heartily does things God's way—no matter what—and then prayerfully leaves the results of her obedience in the hands of her wise, powerful, and good God. It's your job as a mother to follow God's plan. It's God's job to work all things together for His divine purposes (Romans 8:28) and prove what is His good and acceptable and perfect will (Romans 12:2) not only in your child's life, but yours, too! A mother trusts and obeys the God she is serving as she raises her children.

An Invitation to Beauty

Obviously my emotions run deep when it comes to mothering. I hope and pray that my passion provides the push needed to bring out the fighter in you! As Mrs. Schaeffer remarked, "Being a mother is worth fighting for!" When it comes to mothering, there is no place for neutrality, ignorance, aloofness, or a hands-thrown-up-in-the-air, "I give up" attitude! That's why I am trying to call up in you the fierce emotions that can compel the constant care, the ongoing efforts, the never-give-up attitude, and the motivation to give 100 percent-plus! Being a mother—God's kind of mother—touches generations and generations of children.

To close, let me tell you that I wept as I read about the mother of the late Bill Bright, founder of Campus Crusade for Christ. She was described as an "ordinary" woman. Yet as she lay dying at age 93, 109 members of her family, including children, grandchildren, great-grandchildren and great-great-grandchildren, made their way to her bedside to express their love and appreciation. All of them wanted to rise up to call her "blessed."[10] And that, my dear, dear friend, is exactly what I want for myself and for you!

-22-

A Crowning Chorus

HER PRAISE

᷄᷄

"Her children rise up and call her blessed,
and her husband also, and he praises her:
'Many daughters have done well,
but you excel them all.'"
Proverbs 31:28-29

I was touched by this husband's loving tribute to his faithful wife in the dedication of a book he wrote:

With deep love and appreciation, I dedicate this book to my beloved partner and wife, Evelyn, who for over four decades has always been by my side to give me love, cooperation, and understanding when others doubted. Through the years she has joined me in mutual devotion and prayer to our Heavenly Father and has helped me keep faith when the vision of others was limited—truly a helpmate given by God.[1]

The words in this dedication reflect the kind of gratitude and appreciation that abides in the heart of the Proverbs 31 woman's husband and sets the stage for this chapter's crowning chorus of praise for the woman who is beautiful in God's eyes.

An Excellent Wife

Not only has the Proverbs 31 woman proved to be a blessed mother, but now we see—not surprisingly—that she's an excellent and appreciated wife, too, who enjoys the sunshine of her husband's approval. In our poem of virtues, the man who has first place in her heart has the last specific word of praise for his beautiful-in-God's-eyes wife.

The finale begins as "her husband also [rises up]" (Proverbs 31:28). This fine woman's children have concluded their commendations, and now the one who matters most speaks. He offers heartfelt words of tribute, recognizing and appreciating all she has done for him. He sings the crowning chorus of praise for the numerous selfless works his beautiful wife has showered him with through the years.

The blessed husband—the great leader of the people and a man of influence who is known in the gates—"praises [his wife]" (Proverbs 31:28)! Proudly and publicly, he lauds the woman who helps bear the burden of his every care; she is his comforter in every distress, his faithful adviser, his best friend, his unceasing joy, and his brightest crown! He who is the companion of her youth (Proverbs 2:17) has shared much of life's journey with her. And here, long after the children have "risen up" and gone out into the world, she continues as his faithful wife, doing him good all the days of her life (verse 12).

An Army of Virtuous Women

In hushed anticipation, we wait as the husband of God's beautiful woman—the person who knows her best—begins his statement of praise: "Many daughters have done well" (Proverbs 31:29). Knowing what a noble woman is and does (after all, he's married to one!), this wise man recognizes that *many* are noble. Indeed, an entire army of good women ("daughters") exists. Sitting in the gates of the city (verse 23), he knows who the women of strong character are in his town. I'm sure he could list the women who have achieved wealth, who merit the regard of the community, and who live their lives in a worthy manner. Yes, there are many!

And he acknowledges that the "many daughters have done *well*" (Proverbs 31:29). Do you remember our definition of *virtuous* from chapter 1? We discovered that the word virtuous or *excellent* means "power of mind and power of body" and accurately describes an army. Here the husband of the Proverbs 31 woman picks up that military image in the word *well*. Many have done virtuously. Many have done excellently. Many have done valiantly. Many have proven their worth. Many have gained riches and wealth. Many have shown great force and power.

The Best of All!

"But," this proud and grateful husband continues, "you excel them all" (Proverbs 31:29). His precious wife is beautiful not only in God's eyes, but in his eyes, too. His chorus of praise resounds as he declares: "You surpass them all! You transcend them all! You far outdo them all! You are better than all of them!"[2] In other words, he points out that other women "do" worthily, but his beautiful wife "is" worthy. Other women "do" their activities (and do them with excellence), but he praises his wife because of her very character: She "is" excellent![3] Comparing her to the complete army of the other virtuous women in God's army, he confidently claims that she is the noblest of women. Captivated by her excellencies, he exults, "You are the best of all!"[4]

Just a note: The Old Testament Hebrew proclaims, "You ascend over all [of] them."[5] This Hebrew wording suggests that the husband gives his blessing in genuine appreciation of his wife's actual accomplishments and activities—not as an act of graciousness, obligation, or well-meaning politeness.

God's beautiful woman truly merits this honest praise because she is indeed the best of all!

A Kaleidoscope of Virtues

Oh, my dear friend, I hope you are not growing weary of this faithful woman who so perfectly exemplifies beauty as God sees it. For 20 verses we've looked at her godly virtues and her sterling character. This great woman is not shallow, nor is her beautiful life built on a thin foundation. Her godly and virtuous beauty permeates her life and her very being, so we can learn much of value from her. Proverbs 20:5 says, "A man [or woman] of understanding will draw [the instruction] out." That's been our purpose throughout this book—to learn all that we can about and from the beauty of the Proverbs 31 woman.

In my mind, she is like a kaleidoscope. As a child, did you ever have a kaleidoscope, a small cardboard tube filled with brightly colored glass or plastic shards? Holding the kaleidoscope up toward the light, you could view the stained-glass patterns fashioned by the shards as the light shined through them. Then, as you turned the kaleidoscope, the many jewel-toned shards changed positions, creating yet another magnificent design of beauty.

Well, my magnificent friend, that's what the woman who is beautiful in God's eyes is like. In Proverbs 31, God allows you and me to view the many rich colors and glorious patterns of her multifaceted life. As we've moved from verse to verse, from virtue to virtue, as we've lifted the character of God's beautiful woman up to the light of His Holy Spirit, He has illumined the brilliance of her virtues. They have burst into an exquisite pattern and then, with a slight change of angle as we've moved to another verse, we've seen yet another splendid display of breathtaking beauty. Proverbs 31 is the study of one woman in all her different roles. Each verse enables us to look at all her virtues, but from a different angle. She is a kaleidoscope of virtues!

Give the Proverbs 31 kaleidoscope a series of twists, and you and I can easily understand why her husband so highly praises his beautiful wife. Marvel at the glory of her multifaceted beauty!

- She adds honor to her husband's name and reputation because she is "a virtuous wife" (verse 10).

- She contributes positively to his financial well-being and manages his money so that "he will have no lack of gain" (verse 11).

- She eases his mind so he can concentrate on the demands of his leadership position: "The heart of her husband safely trusts her. . . . She does him good and not evil all the days of her life" (verses 11 and 12).

- She provides for the needs at home, "[rising] while it is yet night and [providing] food for her household" (verse 15).

- She increases his assets and expands his property: "From her profits [she buys a field] and plants a vineyard" (verse 16).

- She counsels and encourages him with the words she speaks: "She opens her mouth with wisdom and on her tongue is the law of kindness" (verse 26).

- She frees him up from worries at home so that he can serve his community. She responsibly "watches over the ways of her household" (verse 27).

- She raises his children and, as a result of her fine efforts, "her children rise up and call her blessed" (verse 28).

No wonder that her husband's crowning chorus of praise for this beautiful-in-God's-eyes woman goes on and on through the centuries!

A Beautiful Crown

And here another image catches our eye. The woman praised in this exuberant chorus is herself a beautiful crown for the one speaking forth the praise! As Proverbs 12:4 says, "An excellent wife is the crown of her husband." God's beautiful wife is the crown her husband wears. She is his brightest ornament, and she draws all eyes to him, as one who is eminently honored and blessed.[6] A crown is a mark of dignity, and a virtuous woman—a person of strength and dignity in her own right (verse 25)—brings respectability, credit, and reputation not to herself, but to her husband.[7] Adorning and beautifying *his* life, *she* is an honor to him. She is his crown.

And God's beautiful woman is pleased to be her husband's crown. Shunning the spotlight, she gladly gives her life behind the scenes so that her husband may be noticed and honored. She is glad when he is the center of attention, when he excels, when he is recognized, when he rises to the top. Indeed, she delights in living in his shadow. His promotion is her greatest reward. She desires that her husband be highly respected and esteemed, so she contentedly offers the supreme sacrifice of herself for him.

This image of the crown offers us one more message: This beautiful crown is a crown of joy. I say that because, in the day of God's beautiful woman, a bridegroom dressed as much like a king as possible for the wedding festivities. If he could afford it, he wore a gold crown. If not, a woven garland of fresh flowers offered him a regal appearance. For that one glorious day, even a peasant seemed a prince as the people paid him the respect called for by the exalted rank which his crown symbolized.[8]

Then, when the wedding day faded away, the festivities were but a memory, and life returned to normal, a man's new wife became his crown. This woman who is beautiful in God's eyes supplies him with the dignity due a king. She has become the symbol of honor for him—a crown to her husband who richly adorns his life and makes his every day a celebration. Thanks to this virtuous woman, the joy of the wedding day has continued throughout his life. This, dear one, is what you and I want to be to our husband—a beautiful crown of dignity and joy for him to wear daily!

But What if . . . ?

Once again, I can hear your heart-cries. You're wondering, "But what if my husband isn't the provider, the husband, the father, the spiritual leader God calls him to be? Why should I bother?" Here's a maxim for both of us: Life's circumstances never negate God's standards. Let me explain what I mean by showing you some beautiful women in God's army who had a difficult marriage.

Hannah—As we learned earlier, Hannah was married to a man with another wife who persecuted and willfully provoked Hannah day after day, year after year (1 Samuel 1). Yet Hannah allowed these difficult circumstances to press her closer to God. As a result, Hannah stands as one of the very few women in Scripture about whom nothing negative is said. Her husband certainly wasn't the leader he should have been, but Hannah did not let her life circumstances negate God's standards for her life or interfere with His desire that she be beautiful in His eyes!

Abigail—You and I also considered the sad life of Abigail (1 Samuel 25). Sentenced to life with a foolish alcoholic husband, Abigail bore down and was the best wife, home manager, and supervisor of the servants she could possibly be. Recognized by them as a virtuous woman, she is the one the servants reported to when her household was in danger. Then, ever virtuous in character, she literally saved the day—and the lives of her husband and his servants, her household and herself.

Esther—Queen Esther, whom I haven't mentioned before in this book, was married to a godless king. Prone to fits of rage and probably an alcoholic, he was a difficult man (see the Book of Esther). Yet Esther (meaning "star") shines forth as another model of a woman who is beautiful in God's eyes. Ten chapters of the Bible are devoted to her humility, courage, and wisdom. She put all her virtues to work to nurture her relationship with her husband and to save the lives of her people, the Jews.

In light of these examples, I urge you to please look beyond your circumstances, *far* beyond your present difficulties, and even beyond your husband. Instead, as you gaze outward, put God's kaleidoscope of virtues up to the light of His bright hope and His shining Word and give it a turn! Behold the beauty He has in mind for you and is maturing in you in the midst of your challenging circumstances. God's grace is sufficient (2 Corinthians 12:9), He is faithful (1 Corinthians 10:13), and He has His good purposes for your life (Romans 8:28)! One of those purposes is to make you even more beautiful in His eyes, more like His own Son Jesus (Romans 8:29)!

In your situation, however, you may be thinking, "What if my husband never praises me? I do all these things on God's Proverbs 31 'to-do' list and I try so hard, but I still never get even a thank you!" I think you know my answer by now: Just like your role as mother to your children, your energy and efforts as a wife must never be motivated by possible rewards.

Again, God has determined your role and Scripture describes it: As wives, you and I are to do what we do "heartily, *as to the Lord* and *not to men*" (Colossians 3:23)—and that "not to men" phrase includes your husband. You are called to give whatever time and effort necessary to be the wife God calls you to be, "hoping for nothing in return" (Luke 6:35). You are called to love and serve and work and watch and get up and stay up and do good all the days of your life (and . . . and . . . and . . . !) because that's what your all-wise, all-loving God asks of you. Your job is to believe in the rightness of His ways and follow through on His plan for beauty, trusting Him for the kind of blessing He chooses to bestow—even if that blessing does not include your husband's praise. Don't let anyone (including your husband) or anything (including a lack of praise) interfere with God's plan for your godly beauty!

Finally, in case you're questioning, "But what if I don't have a husband?" please don't forget that the emphasis throughout this book is on virtues, on godly character, on who you *are*—not on whether or not you are married or have children. God wants all of His women to be beautifully virtuous in His eyes—and that includes *you!*

An Invitation to Beauty

We're standing near the top of the mountain of virtues we began climbing so many chapters ago! But before we take our final step or two, whisper a prayer now and walk with me through this checklist for beauty.

As a woman—Do you put the power of your mind and body to work on behalf of your husband, family, and home? At the same time, is it your deepest purpose to not only *do* worthily, but to *be* a worthy woman, consistently exemplary in character?

As a homemaker—Do you provide for the needs at home? Do you carefully and attentively look over the ways of your household?

As a mother—Are you raising your husband's children to love and serve the Lord, thereby giving your husband peace of mind and strengthening his reputation in the community?

As a wife—Does your behavior give honor to your husband's name and reputation? Do you contribute positively to his financial well-being through careful management of the household finances? Does your husband trust in you and your faithfulness? Do your words encourage and build him up for the demands of life? In your honest opinion, has your husband found a virtuous woman in you, a woman who is beautiful in God's eyes? Pray that he has—and keep pursuing the heights of excellence!

-23-

A Spirit of Reverence
HER FAITH

∽

"Charm is deceitful and beauty is vain,
but a woman who fears the Lord,
she shall be praised."
Proverbs 31:30

We've done it! We've made it to the pinnacle of virtue, the goal of the climb we began together in chapter 1—and we have come a long way! Now, finally, *finally*, in this book about beauty, we reach the summit and there discover a verse that actually contains the word "beauty"!

But wait a minute! What this verse says about beauty is not what we might have expected at the start! We've climbed toward the pinnacle of godly beauty only to realize that it is *not* what we've been told all our lives!

Here the message of Proverbs 31 comes into sharp focus, and we see God's truth one more time: This rich, life-changing Old Testament chapter is all about what is beautiful in *God's* eyes—not man's eyes, not the world's eyes, not the media's eyes, not an artist's eyes, but *God's* eyes! As we have acknowledged from the beginning of this primer on beauty, God declares, "My thoughts are not your thoughts, nor are your ways My ways. . . . My ways are higher than your ways, and My thoughts than your thoughts" (Isaiah 55:8-9).

And here we have God's specific thoughts on beauty: "Charm is deceitful and beauty is vain, but a woman who fears the Lord, she shall be praised" (Proverbs 31:30).

It has certainly been instructive to sit in on the lessons of young Lemuel as his wise mother has tutored him along through an alphabet of true feminine beauty. At this point of his lessons, he knows the kind of woman he should look for as a partner for life—and you and I know what God's standards for our lives are. Now this mother, who cares oh-so-deeply about her son's future and who knows what is most important in this life, speaks again. Hear what she has to say about exactly what is—and is not—beautiful in a woman.

The Twin Vanities of Charm and Beauty

"Charm is deceitful," Proverbs 31:30 declares. Warning her son (and all who will heed her wisdom), our teacher cries out, "Don't desire what is charming! Don't fall for charm! Charm is deceitful. Charm is fickle. Charm is fleeting. In the end, charm is one of life's illusions, one of life's vanities!" Charm may indeed lure and fascinate, but it can never produce happiness or get the work of life done. Perhaps in the back of this concerned mom's mind was the proverb that condemns "getting treasures by a lying [charming, deceitful] tongue" (Proverbs 21:6).

"And beauty is vain," she adds (Proverbs 31:30). Still sounding the alarm, our teacher continues: "And don't be fooled by looks! Remember that beauty is only skin deep. Beauty is fleeting, fading—nothing but a vapor!" Although everyone appreciates loveliness of form, physical beauty is transitory and temporary. It can also be misleading and even dangerous. And, like its twin sister charm, beauty does not guarantee a happy life. Neither does beauty alone effectively manage the nuts-and-bolts reality of life.

A Love for the Lord

Throughout this book about beauty, you and I have looked closely at the character qualities of the Proverbs 31 woman and at the many activities that fill her busy life. We've looked at her the way we look at a watch, seeing her moving hands and looking for their message to us. But now, dear friend, we are allowed to see what's inside that makes her tick. Where does her love come from? What is the source of her selflessness . . . her mercy . . . her remarkable energy? What guides her, giving her purpose and defining her goals? What makes it possible for this wonder-full woman to be such a solid rock? Where does she find the deep motivation to give herself to such noble efforts for a lifetime? What makes her so beautiful in God's eyes?

The answer is right here in Proverbs 31:30, our final step in understanding God's beauty. Key to all that this beautiful-in-God's-eyes woman is and does is *God Himself*! Proverbs 31:30 is very specific: "A woman who fears the Lord, she shall be praised." You see, God's beautiful woman is a woman who loves Him, who "fears the Lord" (Proverbs 31:30)! He finds it beautiful that she takes Him seriously and takes obedience to His Word seriously.

What exactly does it mean to "fear" the Lord? I hear this question often. In simple terms, a woman who fears the Lord is a woman whose spiritual commitment to God is a total commitment.

How can you nurture your commitment to the Lord and become more beautiful in His eyes? Being beautiful in God's eyes calls for you to focus on your inner character instead of your external appearance. Rather than the clothes you wear, the hairstyle you choose, the car you drive, or the house you decorate, you are to be primarily concerned about living out the holy character that God works in you as you live in His presence. You are to seek the praise of God rather than men.

You are to shun the transitory vanities of this world and pursue instead the eternal beauty of the Lord. These—not face and form—are the interests of a woman who fears the Lord. It is your fear of the Lord that sanctifies every other part of your life and shows the internal majesty of God that is at your very core.

What difference does such a deep commitment to the Lord make? Put simply, it influences all that you and I do! Just as the sun radiates its light, so the presence of the Lord shines through in all you do and in the dedication with which you do it, bringing light to all you touch. Just as fountains, springs, and waterfalls are fed by a source, so your joyous, refreshing power and purposes issue forth from your deep-seated commitment to God. When your heart trusts in God, you refresh the people around you with your selfless deeds and dedication. Your supreme love for God energizes your conduct, your character, and your love for others. Your faith in God generates, animates, and adorns the beauty of your moral stature and the usefulness of your life.

The How-To's of Beauty

God's garland of praise is reserved for the woman who believes in God and walks faithfully in His ways. After all, "The fear of the Lord is the beginning of knowledge" (Proverbs 1:7), and we've seen again and again that the woman who is beautiful in God's eyes is wise as well as beautiful in spirit. The good news is that you and I can know her kind—God's kind—of beauty. How?

1. *More love to Thee, O Christ*—In our New Testament day and age, a woman who is beautiful in God's eyes enjoys a personal relationship with God through His Son, Jesus Christ. That's why, over and over again throughout this book, I have pointed to Colossians 3:23—"Whatever you do,

do it heartily, *as to the Lord* and not to men." When Jesus
Christ rules your heart and life, then all that you do is an act
of worship. It is this kind of love for Christ that makes you
truly beautiful in God's eyes!

Again, you and I live out our fear of the Lord through our
relationship to God's Son, Jesus Christ. Therefore, God's
greatest question to you (and mine, too) is "Do you know
Jesus Christ as your Savior and Lord?" Your faith in Him is
key to being beautiful in God's eyes.

2. Schedule time with the Lord—Anyone who is not fully
convinced of their need to seek the Lord regularly usually
doesn't! I certainly hope that, by this point in our climb, you
realize that you need to seek the Lord if you are to do the job
to which He has called you.

Speaking of spending time with the Lord, I just looked at
my schedule for this week. It includes such exciting appointments as a teeth cleaning at the dentist and the delivery of
our drinking water. You and I schedule nonessentials of life
like these, so don't you think we should schedule time with
the Lord?

Take a look at your own schedule. When are your
appointments with the Lord? What additional time with
Him can you plan? Your faith is nurtured and strengthened
when you spend sweet minutes reading your Bible and
hushed in prayer. You've read much in this book about time
management, organization, goals, and scheduling. Now use
these lessons and skills to ensure that you are spending the
life-giving, life-changing, life-beautifying time with God that
you need!

As one who names Jesus as Lord, you are privileged to be
able to behold the beauty of the Lord (Psalm 27:4) and worship the Lord in the beauty of His holiness (Psalm 29:2).

When you do, His beauty becomes your beauty, and your life bears the mark of a woman who fears the Lord.

3. *Embrace God's plan*—A poem of praise for a virtuous woman, Proverbs 31 lays out God's plan for your life and mine. Just to review, God calls you to be a woman of character, a faithful wife (if you're married) and devoted mother, a dedicated home-builder, and a confident woman because of your reverent fear of the Lord. Rather than resist God's perfect design, I invite you to embrace it, to glory in it, to delight in its every aspect, to excel in it, and to experience its beauty. A woman who fears the Lord is a woman who takes seriously God, His Word, and His plan. When you wholeheartedly embrace God's beautiful plan for your life as the Proverbs 31 woman does, you will be clothed—as she is—with strength and dignity, no matter what comes your way.

4. *Do your best*—The woman of Proverbs 31 is strong and physically fit. We don't know what she looked like, but we can be sure that she did her best. We also know that she dressed dramatically in garments of regal purple, but because of her magnificent virtues we can also be sure that she wasn't overly concerned about her appearance. She did, however, bring honor to her husband's name. Clearly, she offers you and me a good guideline: Do what you need to do to be healthy and fit and to bring honor to your family.

How will you know if you are too concerned about your physical beauty? I'll let two of God's beautiful women of our day share their thoughts in response to that difficult question.

Author Anne Ortlund came to this conclusion: "I noticed that twenty-two verses [of Proverbs 31] describe this woman's kindness, godliness, hard work, loving relationships—and only one verse out of the twenty-two [verse 22] describes how she looked. . . . Seeing this kind of proportion in Proverbs 31 . . . I prayed, 'O Father, I want to give 1/22 of my time to making myself as outwardly beautiful as I can; and I want to give all the rest of my time, 21/22 of my life, to becoming wise, kind, godly, hard-working, and the rest.'"[1]

When another woman I know prayed about nurturing a heart that fears the Lord, she decided to make the commitment of a daily "time tithe." In other words, she sets apart one-tenth of her waking hours for prayer and Bible study.

Figure out for yourself a formula that balances nurturing in God's presence an inner beauty that pleases Him and the demands of your daily life. Always remember that the time, energy, and attention you give to your relationship with the Lord is attention to inner, godly, and *true beauty*!

An Invitation to Beauty

In case you're not sure about how to have a relationship with Jesus Christ, let me invite you to establish one today and so begin living a life of true internal, eternal beauty! You can set foot on the path of growing in godly beauty right now by earnestly praying these words:

> Jesus, I know I am a sinner, but I want to repent of my sins and turn to follow You. I believe that You died for my sins and rose again victorious over the power of sin and death. I want to accept You as my personal Savior. Come into my life, Lord Jesus, and help me obey You from this day forward.

I'm praying for you right now! True beauty—indeed, all beauty—begins in Jesus Christ!

-24-

The Harvest of a Lifetime
HER REWARD

cↄ

"Give her of the fruit of her hands,
and let her own works praise her in the gates."
Proverbs 31:31

A modern-day "proverb" sums up the path of the Christian life: "The way up is down!" Keep this saying in mind as you consider this final verse from Proverbs 31—the verse that closes the Book of Proverbs. I think those five words aptly describe the life of our beautiful lady, the Proverbs 31 woman. For her, the way up was down.

The woman who is beautiful in God's eyes, whose life and work we've been looking at for 22 verses and 24 chapters, has chosen to live her life in the shadows and to bear fruit that grows only in the shade. Hidden at home, she gives her utmost for God's highest glory as a woman who fears the Lord (Proverbs 31:30). Oh, she (like you) does things outside the home as well, but inside the home no task is too meaningless or effort too small to merit her most excellent endeavor. Now we see the rewards that await the one who has long been content to silently serve: A loud and unanimous chorus of praise celebrates the woman who chose the way down.

The Fruit of Her Hands

As young Lemuel's mother ends her lessons, she looks deeply into her son's eyes and gives one more word of instruction: "Give her of the fruit of her hands" (Proverbs 31:31). Just as admirers award conquerors prizes for their feats and prowess, so we too are to give God's beautiful woman her prizes. Paraphrased in today's words, Proverbs 31:31 could read, "Give her credit for her achievements! Give her all that she has earned! Give her all that she has worked for so diligently! Give her the fruit of her hands, the harvest of a lifetime of loving effort! Give her the profit she's earned, the goods she's worked, the reputation she's established, the marriage she's nurtured, the home she's built, the family life she's cultivated, the future she's labored for! Give it all to her!" And, my dear beautiful friend, you and I are called by these final words, too, to give the woman who is beautiful in God's eyes her rewards, a harvest of praise.

And this is indeed a serious call to praise. Too many women are jealous of this woman who is beautiful in God's eyes. They disdain her, even despise her and jeer at her! I've heard her called "mousy," a wall-flower, "just a housewife," a cave woman, and a slave. Some are quick to say, "Look at all her talent! It's such a shame it's wasted at home! Think how far she could rise in the corporate world with her abilities! Poor thing! What a waste!"

This kind of thinking could not be further from the point of the message that God (and His beautiful woman) offers! In fact, as one scholar concludes, "This verse forms a fitting conclusion to what is the most remarkable exposition in the Old Testament on the position of women, exalting . . . her functions in the home as wife, mother, and mistress, and showing how contentedness and happiness in the domestic circle depend upon the foresight and oversight of this queen of the hearth."[1]

Far from pitying the Proverbs 31 woman, God calls us to praise her, admire her, and follow her—indeed, to become her! You see, as a woman who fears the Lord, *she* shall be praised (Proverbs 31:29)!

Praise in the Gates

Proverbs 31:31 exults, "Let her own works praise her in the gates." These words are an interesting twist to what has come earlier in Proverbs 31. Do you remember looking at the husband of God's beautiful woman and seeing his prominent position in the gates of the city as a lawyer and leader (verse 23)? Well, now we see his wife's position of honor in the gates as well. Others are talking about her in public places. They are praising her for her works—which themselves praise her, too. How lovely and how encouraging to see that where men congregate, where the leaders of the people meet in solemn assembly, her praise is sung and the highest honor ascribed to her!

We've seen her selflessness, her behind-the-scenes work, and her seemingly unnoticed efforts, but here we learn that her deeds are publicly acknowledged and acclaimed. Like her husband, she enjoys a good reputation and a high standing in the community. Although many of her activities are confined to the home, due recognition of the vital contribution she makes to the community is offered publicly in the gates. As one saint marvels, "Much of what . . . women do is in a supportive role, but imagine what would happen to a building if its support pillars were removed!"[2] Yes, the contributions which the Proverbs 31 woman makes to her husband, her children, her household, her community are necessary and praiseworthy!

But young Lemuel's mother says, "Let her own *works* praise her." Even if all voices were silent, even if no words of praise were spoken, the woman who is beautiful in God's eyes would receive the honor due her: Her very works are a monument to her name. The works of her hands and the fruit of her labor find a voice and proclaim her praise! As our poem declared earlier, "A woman who fears the Lord, she shall be praised" (Proverbs 31:29)—no matter what!

An Invitation to Beauty

O what joy! What glory! What a wonderful harvest of praise! Every voice possible is praising our woman who is so very beautiful in God's eyes! The voice of her children sounds out her praise (verse 28). The voice of her husband issues forth praise (verses 28, 29, 31—his is one of the voices in the gates!). The voice of God praises her (verse 30—the fear of the Lord results in *His* praise!).[3] The voice of other people praises her (verse 31—all those in the gates). Even the voice of her works praises her (verse 31). I, Elizabeth George, praise our Proverbs 31 friend, too. Indeed I've done so for 24 chapters! The only voice not heard is that of the woman herself. She wisely lives out yet another proverb—"Let another man praise you, and not your own mouth" (Proverbs 27:2).

But there is one more voice I want to hear praising God's beautiful woman—and that is yours! I am most interested in you and your praise because the rich beauty of the Proverbs 31 woman is not appreciated by our culture. Our enemy Satan and the fallen world in which we live have painted her beauty as something undesirable, unimportant, and even useless. Oh, how very wrong they are! This woman of Proverbs 31, dear friend and follower of God, is true beauty: She lives out all that is beautiful in God's eyes.

So I call you to praise her! Your praise will indicate that you comprehend the splendor of all that is beautiful in God's eyes. And the richest kind of praise you can offer is to follow in her footsteps. Then my heart will rejoice knowing that you, my companion for so long, are well on your way to becoming beautiful in God's eyes!

Won't you bow your head now and offer your voice, too, in praise to God for His beautiful woman? She is indeed one of His beautiful gifts to you. She is here in Proverbs·31 to inspire, instruct, and encourage you when you fail, when you find your vision dimming, or when you sense your priorities shifting. A fresh visit with the woman who is beautiful in God's eyes will renew your vision, restore your strength, and rekindle your love for God and your commitment to His plan for making you and your life beautiful in His eyes!

Notes

 ᴄ᷉᷉᷉᷉

CHAPTER 1

1. C. F. Keil & F. Delitzsch, *Commentary on the Old Testament, Vol. 6* (Grand Rapids, MI: William B. Eerdmans Publishing Company, 1975), p. 327.
2. James Strong, *Exhaustive Concordance of the Bible* (Nashville: Abingdon Press, 1973), p. 39.
3. Edith Schaeffer, *Common Sense Christian Living* (Nashville: Thomas Nelson Publishers, 1983), p. 108.

CHAPTER 2

1. Curtis Vaughan, ed., *The Old Testament Books of Poetry from 26 Translations*—The Bible in Basic English (Grand Rapids MI: Zondervan Bible Publishers, 1973), p. 629.
2. Vaughan, *Old Testament Books of Poetry*, The American Standard Version, p. 629.
3. *The Encyclopedia Americana, Vol. 23* (New York: Americana Corporation, 1958), p. 750.
4. Vaughan, *Old Testament Books of Poetry*, New American Standard Bible, p. 630.
5. *The Encyclopedia Americana, Vol. 21*, pp. 454-56.
6. Vaughan, *Old Testament Books of Poetry*, Rotherham, p. 629.
7. *The Encyclopedia Americana, Vol. 7*, pp. 676-77.
8. *Our Daily Bread*, Radio Bible Class Ministries, Grand Rapids, MI, May, 1982.

CHAPTER 3

1. Cheryl Julia Dunn, *A Study of Proverbs 31:10-31*, Master thesis (Biola University, 1993), p. 27.
2. Ibid., p. 27.
3. Ibid., pp. 25-26.
4. Curtis Vaughan, ed., *The Old Testament Books of Poetry from 26 Translations*—The Bible in Basic English (Grand Rapids, MI: Zondervan Bible Publishers, 1973), pp. 629-30.

CHAPTER 4

1. "Building Your Nest Egg," by Deborah Adamson, *Los Angeles Daily News*, April 20, 1997.
2. Cheryl Julia Dunn, *A Study of Proverbs 31:10-31*, Master thesis (Biola University, 1993), p. 25.
3. Barbara Gilder Quint, *Family Circle*, May 29, 1984. (Condensed in *Reader's Digest*.)

CHAPTER 5

1. Merrill F. Unger, *Unger's Bible Dictionary* (Chicago: Moody Press, 1972), p. 313.
2. Cheryl Julia Dunn, *A Study of Proverbs 31:10-31*, Master thesis (Biola University, 1993), p. 31.
3. Robert L. Alden, *Proverbs, A Commentary on an Ancient Book of Timeless Advice* (Grand Rapids, MI: Baker Book House, 1990), p. 220.
4. Mrs. Charles E. Cowman, *Streams in the Desert, Volumes 1 and 2* (Grand Rapids, MI: Zondervan Publishing House, original publishing date 1925, reprinted 1965 and 1966 respectively).
5. Ray Beeson and Ranelda Mack Hunsicker, *The Hidden Price of Greatness* (Wheaton, IL: Tyndale House Publishers, Inc., 1991), pp. 97-107.
6. Anne Ortlund, *Building a Great Marriage* (Old Tappan, NJ: Fleming H. Revell Company, 1984), page unknown. (Prayer written by Temple Gairdner, nineteenth century Scottish missionary and scholar.)

CHAPTER 6

1. James M. Freeman, *Manners and Customs of the Bible* (Plainfield, NJ: Logos International, 1972), p. 198.
2. W. O. E. Oesterley, *The Book of Proverbs* (London: Methuen and Company, Ltd., 1929), p. 284.
3. C. F. Keil and F. Delitzsch, *Commentary on the Old Testament—Vol. 6* (Grand Rapids, MI: William B. Eerdmans Publishing Company, 1975), p. 329.
4. Fred H. Wight, *Manners and Customs of Bible Lands* (Chicago: Moody Press, 1978), p. 83.
5. G. M. Mackie, *Bible Manners and Customs* (Old Tappan, NJ: Fleming H. Revell Company, no date given), p. 59.
6. Cheryl Julia Dunn, *A Study of Proverbs 31:10-31*, Master thesis (Biola University, 1993), p. 38.
7. G. M. Mackie, *Bible Manners and Customs*, p. 667.
8. Ibid.
9. Thomas Kinkade, *Simpler Times* (Eugene, OR: Harvest House Publishers, 1996), p. 69.
10. Edith Schaeffer, *Common Sense Christian Living* (Nashville: Thomas Nelson Publishers, 1983), pp. 88-89.

CHAPTER 7

1. Curtis Vaughan, ed., *The Old Testament Books of Poetry from 26 Translations*—Lamsa (Grand Rapids, MI: Zondervan Bible Publishers, 1973), p. 630.
2. Gene Getz, *The Measure of a Woman* (Glendale, CA: Regal Books, 1977), p. 125.
3. Elizabeth George, *Loving God with All Your Mind* (Eugene, OR: Harvest House Publishers, 1994).

CHAPTER 8

1. Curtis Vaughan, ed., *The Old Testament Books of Poetry from 26 Translations*—Lamsa (Grand Rapids, MI: Zondervan Bible Publishers, 1973), p. 630.
2. James M. Freeman, *Manners and Customs of the Bible* (Plainfield, NJ: Logos International, 1972), p. 50.
3. G. M. Mackie, *Bible Manners and Customs* (Old Tappan, NJ: Fleming H. Revell Company, no date given), p. 99.
4. Cheryl Julia Dunn, *A Study of Proverbs 31:10-31*, Master thesis (Biola University, 1993), pp. 52-53.
5. Ibid., pp. 51-53.
6. Ibid., p. 51.
7. Ibid.
8. Ibid., pp. 51-52.
9. Lucinda Secrest McDowell, "This I Carry with Me Always," *Christian Parenting Today*, May/June, 1993, pp. 22-23.
10. Alan Lakein, *How to Get Control of Your Time and Your Life* (New York: Signet Books, 1974), p. 46.
11. Edwin C. Bliss, *Getting Things Done* (New York: Charles Scribner's Sons, 1976), pp. 148-49.

CHAPTER 9

1. *Webster's New Collegiate Dictionary* (Springfield, MA: G. & C. Merriam Co., Publishers, 1961), p. 954.
2. Robert L. Alden, *Proverbs, A Commentary on an Ancient Book of Timeless Advice* (Grand Rapids, MI: Baker Book House, 1990), p. 220.
3. C. F. Keil and F. Delitzsch, *Commentary on the Old Testament—Vol. VI* (Grand Rapids, MI: William B. Eerdmans Publishing Company, 1975), p. 330.
4. Crawford H. Toy, *A Critical and Exegetical Commentary on the Book of Proverbs* (Edinburgh: T. & T. Clark, 1899), p. 544.
5. Cheryl Julia Dunn, *A Study of Proverbs 31:10-31*, Master thesis (Biola University, 1993), pp. 58-59.

6. *The Living Bible: Paraphrased,* by Kenneth Taylor (Wheaton, IL: Tyndale House Publishers, 1971).
7. Edith Schaeffer, *Hidden Art* (Wheaton, IL: Tyndale House Publishers, 1971).

Chapter 10

1. Crawford H. Toy, *A Critical and Exegetical Commentary on the Book of Proverbs* (Edinburgh: T. & T. Clark, 1899), p. 544.
2. William McKane, *Proverbs, A New Approach* (Philadelphia: The Westminster Press, 1970), p. 668.
3. Cheryl Julia Dunn, *A Study of Proverbs 31:10-31,* Master thesis (Biola University, 1993), p. 64.
4. Ibid.
5. Ibid., pp. 63-65.
6. Curtis Vaughan, ed., *The Old Testament Books of Poetry from 26 Translations*—Knox (Grand Rapids, MI: Zondervan Bible Publishers, 1973), p. 630.
7. Sir Alexander Paterson, *United Evangelical Action,* Fall, 1975, p. 27.
8. "You," by Mac-Sim-Ology.

Chapter 11

1. William McKane, *Proverbs, A New Approach* (Philadelphia: The Westminster Press, 1970), p. 668.
2. Ted W. Engstrom, *The Pursuit of Excellence* (Grand Rapids, MI: Zondervan Publishing House, 1982), p. 36.

Chapter 12

1. C. F. Keil and F. Delitzsch, *Commentary on the Old Testament, Vol. 6* (Grand Rapids, MI: William B. Eerdmans Publishing Company, 1975), p. 332.
2. Sybil Stanton, *The 25 Hour Woman* (Old Tappan, NJ: Fleming H. Revell Company, 1986), p. 169.
3. Anne Ortlund, *The Disciplines of the Beautiful Woman* (Waco, TX: Word, Incorporated, 1977), pp. 66-67.
4. Ted W. Engstrom, *The Pursuit of Excellence* (Grand Rapids, MI: Zondervan Publishing House, 1982), p. 33.
5. Ruth Wagner Miller, "The Time Minder" (*Christian Herald,* 1980), pp. 76-77.
6. "A Woman's Love" by Douglas Malloch.

Chapter 13

1. Cheryl Julia Dunn, *A Study of Proverbs 31:10-31,* Master thesis (Biola University, 1993), p. 36.

2. Barbara Keener Shenk, *The God of Sarah*, Rebekah and Rachel (Scottdale, PA: Herald Press, 1985), p. 127.
3. Dunn, *Study of Proverbs 31:10-31*, p. 85.
4. David Thomas, *Book of Proverbs Expository and Homiletical Commentary* (Grand Rapids, MI: Kregel Publications, 1982), p. 793.
5. Ibid.
6. Edith Schaeffer, *Hidden Art* (Wheaton, IL: Tyndale House Publishers, 1971), pp. 128-32.
7. Stanley High, *Billy Graham* (New York: McGraw Hill, 1956), p. 127.

CHAPTER 14

1. C. F. Keil and F. Delitzsch, *Commentary on the Old Testament—Vol. 6* (Grand Rapids, MI: William B. Eerdmans Publishing Company, 1975), p. 334.
2. William McKane, *Proverbs, A New Approach* (Philadelphia: The Westminster Press, 1970), p. 669.
3. Keil and Delitzsch, *Commentary on the Old Testament—Vol. 6*, p. 335.
4. Crawford H. Toy, *The Book of Proverbs* (Edinburgh: T. & T. Clark, 1899), p. 545.
5. W. O. E. Oesterley, *The Book of Proverbs* (London: Methuen & Co., Ltd., 1929), p. 285.

CHAPTER 15

1. Curtis Vaughan, ed., *The Old Testament Books of Poetry from 26 Translations* (Grand Rapids, MI: Zondervan Bible Publishers, 1973), p. 631.
2. Vaughan, *Old Testament Books of Poetry*, The Jerusalem Bible, p. 631.
3. Cheryl Julia Dunn, *A Study of Proverbs 31:10-31*, Master thesis (Biola University, 1993), p. 101.
4. Ibid., p. 102.
5. Robert L. Alden, *Proverbs, A Commentary on an Ancient Book of Timeless Advice* (Grand Rapids, MI: Baker Book House, 1990), p. 221.
6. Linda Dillow, *Creative Counterpart* (Nashville: Thomas Nelson, Inc., Publishers, 1977), p. 23.
7. Denis Waitley, *Seeds of Greatness* (Old Tappan, NJ: Fleming H. Revell Company, 1983), p. 77.

CHAPTER 16

1. John MacArthur, "God's High Calling for Women," Part 4 (Panorama City, CA: Word of Grace, #GC-54-17, 1986).
2. George Lawson, *Proverbs* (Grand Rapids, MI: Kregel Publications, 1980), p. 883.

3. Donald Hunt, *Pondering the Proverbs* (Joplin, MO: College Press, 1974), p. 432.
4. William J. Peterson, *Martin Luther Had a Wife* (Wheaton, IL: Tyndale House Publishers, Inc., 1983), p. 34.
5. *The Amplified Bible* (Grand Rapids, MI: Zondervan Publishing House, 1970), p. 302.
6. Verna Birkey, *Seminar Workshops for Women* (P.O. Box 3039, Kent, WA 98031), 1979, p. 131.

CHAPTER 17

1. Cheryl Julia Dunn, *A Study of Proverbs 31:10-31*, Master thesis (Biola University, 1993), p. 125.
2. Elizabeth George, *Loving God with All Your Mind, God's Garden of Grace, A Woman After God's Own Heart* (Eugene, OR: Harvest House Publishers, 1994, 1996, 1997 respectively).
3. Edward H. Griggs.

CHAPTER 18

1. Curtis Vaughan, ed., *The Old Testament Books of Poetry from 26 Translations*—The American Standard Version (Grand Rapids, MI: Zondervan Bible Publishers, 1973), p. 632.
2. Cheryl Julia Dunn, *A Study of Proverbs 31:10-31*, Master thesis (Biola University, 1993), p. 126
3. Charles Caldwell Ryrie, *The Ryrie Study Bible* (Chicago: Moody Press, 1978), p. 984.
4. Vaughan, *Old Testament Books of Poetry*, The American Standard Version, p. 632.
5. Ray and Anne Ortlund, *The Best Half of Life* (Glendale, CA: Regal Books, 1976), p. 88.
6. Stephen B. Douglass, *Managing Yourself* (San Bernardino, CA: Here's Life Publishers, Inc., 1978). For an expanded treatment of these categories, read Elizabeth George, *Life Management for Busy People* (Eugene, OR: Harvest House Publishers, 2002).
7. *Great Hymns of the Faith*, "Great Is Thy Faithfulness," by William M. Runyan, 1923.
8. Elizabeth George, *Loving God with All Your Mind* (Eugene, OR: Harvest House Publishers, 1994).
9. Abigail Van Buren, "Dear Abby," *Los Angeles Times*, January 1, 1995.

CHAPTER 19

1. Curtis Vaughan, ed., *The Old Testament Books of Poetry from 26 Translations*—The American Standard Version (Grand Rapids, MI: Zondervan Bible Publishers, 1973), p. 632.

2. Charles Caldwell Ryrie, *The Ryrie Study Bible* (Chicago: Moody Press, 1978), p. 938.

3. Cheryl Julia Dunn, *A Study of Proverbs 31:10-31*, Master thesis (Biola University, 1993), p. 139.

4. H. D. M. Spence and Joseph S. Exell, eds., *The Pulpit Commentary—Vol. 9* (Grand Rapids, MI: William B. Eerdmans Publishing Company, 1978), p. 601.

5. Dunn, *Study of Proverbs 31:10-31*, p. 139.

6. *Life Application Bible* (Wheaton, IL: Tyndale House Publishers, 1988), p. 449.

7. Elizabeth George, *A Woman After God's Own Heart* (Eugene, OR: Harvest House Publishers, 1997), pp. 38-39.

8. William MacDonald, *Enjoying the Proverbs* (Kansas City, KS: Walterick Publishers, 1982), p. 86.

9. William MacDonald, *Enjoying the Proverbs*, p. 99.

10. Vaughan, *Old Testament Books of Poetry*, The American Standard Version, p. 632.

CHAPTER 20

1. Merrill C. Tenney, ed., *The Zondervan Pictorial Encyclopedia of the Bible*, Vol. 5 (Grand Rapids, MI: Zondervan Publishing House, 1975), pp. 901-02.

2. Cheryl Julia Dunn, *A Study of Proverbs 31:10-31*, Master thesis (Biola University, 1993), p. 144.

3. William McKane, *Proverbs, A New Approach* (Philadelphia: The Westminster Press, 1970), p. 670.

4. Derek Kidner, *The Proverbs* (Downers Grove, IL: InterVarsity Press, 1973), p. 71.

5. Dunn, *Study of Proverbs 31:10-31*, p. 144.

6. Curtis Vaughan, ed., *The Old Testament Books of Poetry from 26 Translations*—Knox (Grand Rapids, MI: Zondervan Bible Publishers, 1973), p. 632.

7. Vaughan, *Old Testament Books of Poetry*, Taylor, p. 632.

8. Edith Schaeffer, *What Is a Family?* (Old Tappan, NJ: Fleming H. Revell Company, 1975), p. 77.

9. Mrs. Isabella Beeton, *Beeton's Book of Household Management* (London: Chancellor Press, 1861).

10. Author unknown.

CHAPTER 21

1. Abraham Cohen, *Proverbs: Hebrew Text and English Translations with an Introduction and Commentary*, (Hindhead, Surrey: The Soncino Press, 1945), p. 214.

2. Ibid.

3. C. F. Keil and F. Delitzsch, *Commentary on the Old Testament—Vol. 6* (Grand Rapids, MI: William B. Eerdmans Publishing Company, 1975), p. 340.

4. W. O. E. Oesterley, *The Book of Proverbs* (London: Methuen and Company, Ltd., 1929), p. 286.

5. Elisabeth Elliot, *The Shaping of a Christian Family* (Nashville: Thomas Nelson Publishers, 1992), p. 201.

6. Edith Schaeffer, *What Is a Family?* (Old Tappan, NJ: Fleming H. Revell Company, 1975), p. 121.

7. E. Schuyler English, *Ordained of the Lord* (Neptune, NJ: Loizeaux Brothers, 1976), p. 35.

8. Elizabeth George, *A Woman After God's Own Heart* (Eugene, OR: Harvest House Publishers, 1997).

9. Schaeffer, *What Is a Family?* p. 92.

10. Vonette Zachary Bright, ed., *The Greatest Lesson I've Ever Learned* (San Bernardino, CA: Here's Life Publishers, Inc., 1991), p. 182.

Chapter 22

1. Robert Gilmour LeTourneau, *Mover of Men and Mountains* (Englewood Cliffs, NJ: Prentice-Hall, 1960).

2. Curtis Vaughan, ed., *The Old Testament Books of Poetry from 26 Translations* (Grand Rapids, MI: Zondervan Bible Publishers, 1973), pp. 632-33.

3. Cheryl Julia Dunn, *A Study of Proverbs 31:10-31*, Master thesis (Biola University, 1993), p. 163.

4. Kenneth Taylor, *The Living Bible* (Wheaton, IL: Tyndale House Publishers, 1971).

5. Ibid.

6. Charles Bridges, rev. by George F. Santa, *A Modern Study in the Book of Proverbs* (Milford, MI: Mott Media, 1978), p. 161.

7. Ralph Wardlaw, *Lectures on the Book of Proverbs—Vol. 3* (Minneapolis, MN: Klock & Klock Christian Publishers, Inc., 1982 reprint), pp. 310-11.

8. Fred H. Wight, *Manners and Customs of Bible Lands* (Chicago: Moody Press, 1953), p. 130.

Chapter 23

1. Anne Ortlund, *The Disciplines of the Beautiful Woman* (Waco, TX: Word Books, 1977), p. 46.

Chapter 24

1. W. O. E. Oesterley, *The Book of Proverbs* (London: Methuen & Company, Ltd., 1929), p. 283.

2. Judy Hubbell, *Messenger*, November 1975, p. 31.

3. Cheryl Julia Dunn, *A Study of Proverbs 31:10-31*, Master thesis (Biola University, 1993), p. 171.

Bibliography

Alden, Robert L. *Proverbs: A Commentary on an Ancient Book of Timeless Advice.* Grand Rapids, MI: Baker Book House, 1983.

Arnot, William. *Studies in Proverbs: Laws from Heaven for Life on Earth.* Grand Rapids, MI: Kregel Publications, 1978.

Dunn, Cheryl Julia. "A Study of Proverbs 31:10-31." Master thesis, Biola University, 1993.

Exell, Joseph S. *Proverbs, The Biblical Illustrator.* Grand Rapids, MI: Baker Book House, 1957.

Hunt, Donald. *Pondering the Proverbs.* Joplin, MO: College Press, 1974.

Ironside, H. A. *Notes on the Book of Proverbs.* New York: Loizeaux Brothers, 1952.

Jamieson, Robert, A. R. Fausset, and David Brown. *Commentary Practical and Explanatory on the Whole Bible.* Grand Rapids, MI: Zondervan Publishing House, 1973.

Karssen, Gien. *The Best of All.* Colorado Springs: NavPress, 1984.

Keil, C.F., and Delitzsch, F. *Commentary on the Old Testament—Vol. 6.* Grand Rapids, MI: William B. Eerdmans Publishing Company, 1975.

Kidner, Derek. *The Proverbs.* The Tyndale Old Testament Commentaries. London: InterVarsity Press, 1973.

Lawson, George. *Proverbs.* Grand Rapids, MI: Kregel Publications, 1980.

MacDonald, William. *Enjoying the Proverbs.* Kansas City, KS: Walterick Publishers, 1965.

McKane, William. *Proverbs: A New Approach.* Philadelphia: The Westminster Press, 1970.

Muffet, Peter. *A Commentary on the Whole Book of Proverbs.* Edinburgh: James Nichol, cir. 1594.

Oesterley, W. O. E. *The Book of Proverbs with Introduction and Notes.* London: Methuen & Co., Ltd., 1929.

Pfeiffer, Charles F. and Everett F. Harrison. *The Wycliffe Bible Commentary.* Chicago: Moody Press, 1973.

Santa, George F. *A Modern Study in the Book of Proverbs: Charles Bridges' Classic Revised for Today's Reader*. Milford, MI: Mott Media, 1978.

Spence, H. D. M. and Joseph S. Exell. *The Pulpit Commentary, Vol. 9, Proverbs, Ecclesiastes, Song of Solomon*. Grand Rapids, MI: William B. Eerdmans Publishing Company, 1978.

Stitzinger, Jim. "Lecture Notes on Proverbs," The Master's Seminary, 1997.

Thomas, David. *Book of Proverbs, Expository and Homiletical Commentary*. Grand Rapids, MI: Kregel Publications, 1982.

Toy, Crawford H. *A Critical and Exegetical Commentary on the Book of Proverbs*, The International Critical Commentary. Edinburgh: T. & T. Clark, 1899.

Wardlaw, Ralph. *Lectures on The Book of Proverbs—Vol. 3*. Minneapolis, MN: Klock & Klock Christian Publishers, Inc., 1982 reprint.

Whybray, R. N. *Proverbs, New Century Bible Commentary*. Grand Rapids, MI: William B. Eerdmans Publishing Company, 1994.

Woodcock, Eldon. *Proverbs, A Topical Study, Bible Study Commentary*. Grand Rapids, MI: Zondervan Publishing House, 1988.

Personal Notes

Personal Notes

_____

_____

_____

_____

_____

_____

_____

_____

_____

_____

_____

_____

_____

_____

_____

_____

_____

_____

_____

_____

_____

Personal Notes

Personal Notes

Personal Notes

Personal Notes

Personal Notes

Personal Notes

_____

_____

_____

_____

_____

_____

_____

_____

_____

_____

_____

_____

_____

_____

_____

_____

_____

_____

Personal Notes

Personal Notes

$\mathcal{I}$f you've benefited from *Beautiful in God's Eyes*, you'll want the companion volume

Beautiful in God's Eyes
Growth and Study Guide

Elizabeth George's brand–new *Beautiful in God's Eyes Growth and Study Guide* provides questions and insights to help women apply the truths of *Beautiful in God's Eyes* to their lives. With practical wisdom, Elizabeth shows women how to triumph over daily pressure and enjoy the creativity, fulfillment, beauty, and purposes God reveals in Proverbs 31 by

- developing a passionate life vision
- making time for family, friends, and God
- improving life–management skills
- keeping their sights on God's plan
- tending to the fires of heart and home

This enlightening study guide encourages women to grow spiritually strong, put their efforts in the right places, and become the active, influential, on–fire believers God wants them to be.

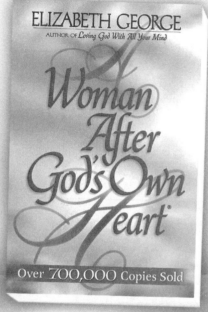

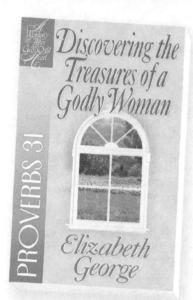

About the Author

Elizabeth George is a bestselling author and speaker whose passion is to teach the Bible in a way that changes women's lives. For information about Elizabeth's books or speaking ministry, to sign up for her mailings, or to share how God has used this book in your life, please write to Elizabeth at:

Elizabeth George
P.O. Box 2879
Belfair, WA 98528

Toll-free fax/phone: 1-800-542-4611
www.ElizabethGeorge.com

orge

ides

ful in God's Eyes
h & Study Guide

Wisdom for a Woman's Life
h & Study Guide

lanagement for Busy Women
h & Study Guide

God with All Your Mind
h & Study Guide

ful Promises for Every
n Growth & Study Guide

emarkable Women of the
Growth & Study Guide

e After God's Own Heart
Study Guide

fter God's Own Heart®
udy Guide

Call to Prayer
ly Guide

gh Calling
ly Guide

alk with God
ly Guide

e

rt